HARRY THE POLIS
THERE'S BEEN A MURDER!

• • •

HARRY MORRIS

BLACK & WHITE PUBLISHING

First published 2010
by Black & White Publishing Ltd
29 Ocean Drive, Edinburgh EH6 6JL

1 3 5 7 9 10 8 6 4 2   10 11 12 13

ISBN 978 1 84502 304 1

A CIP catalogue record for this book is available from the British Library.

Typeset by RefineCatch Ltd, Bungay, Suffolk

Printed in the UK by J F Print Ltd, Sparkford, Somerset

...

This book dedication is long overdue.

Dedicated to Marion Davren
(Love ya my babes!)

...

Also available from Harry the Polis:

Even the Lies Are True
Even More Lies
Nuthin' Like the Truth
Ye're Never Gonnae Believe It!
Aye, That Will Be Right!
Ah Cannae Tell a Lie
Up Tae My Neck in Paperwork
Look Who's Up For A Blether
(DVD LIVE AUDIO PERFORMANCE)

Memories Won't Leave Me

...

The call went out and I raced to the scene
Another RTA where a drunk driver had been.
A girl was bleeding from a cut in her head
Her mother was trapped, appeared to be dead.
Out of nowhere he came with headlights full
Ignoring the stop signs and the red light rule.
He collided full on with their oncoming car
Discarding metal and glass all over the tar.
The fuel flowing freely was a terrifying sight
Within minutes of seeing it, the car was alight.
Pulling the girl from the wreck I tried to return
But flames forced me back and I watched it burn.
Drunk driving was to blame for the loss of a life
This mother of three children and a loving wife.
She'll be laid to rest and he'll be sentenced to jail
But two families will suffer as a result of this tale.
For he also has a family, being a father of five
But neglected them all, to drink and drive!

Someone once told me:

'You don't stop laughing because you grow old.
You actually grow old because you've stopped laughing!'

Well start laughing now! Let's see if we can reverse the
ageing process.

Contents

. . .

PART FIVE

Introduction

• • •

I'm constantly asked the same questions by friends, acquaintances and ex-colleagues: 'Don't you miss the police force, Harry? The harmony, the camaraderie, the laughs with the guys on the shift, the buzz of excitement you feel in your stomach when you're involved in a good bust, culminating with the bad guys getting charged and locked up in a cell?'

My answer to this is always the same. That part of my life has gone; I'm retired from it and you have to move on to the next chapter in your life.

So, as an author with several books published by Black & White, I'm thoroughly enjoying life in my new career.

Here is another collection of my short stories, jokes, anecdotes, tales (and lies) about life. They are not to be taken seriously, but intended to entertain, make you reminisce and bring a smile to your face.

My 'Harry the Polis' series of books is designed to jog your memory, make you laugh and relate a funny story, joke or anecdote to someone who needs to stretch their laughter lines!

Let's face it, we all know some poor bugger who needs a wee laugh now and again! So remember:
'LAUGHTER: THE BEST MEDICINE TO TAKE!'
And best of all, you can never overdose on it either.

Harry

Half-Mast Troosers

· · ·

You've probably noticed in passing the latest trend of the younger men in our society, who wear their denim jeans at half mast, with the rear pockets level with the bend in their knees.

Personally, I think it is one of the most ridiculous styles I've seen. Call me old-fashioned, but that's just my opinion.

Therefore, I was absolutely delighted to be informed of an incident whereby the low wearing of denims was instrumental in the commission of a crime.

It appears a young police officer, off to meet up with some other young cops for a night out up the city centre, stopped off to use cash machine to get some money.

As he shuffled over to it, with his jeans hanging at half mast, he withdrew his wallet and inserted his bank card, not forgetting to look around before entering his PIN number.

Just as he did so, he looked around to see another young male walk up and queue directly behind him.

Turning back to the cash machine, his bank card was returned followed by his cash request. He took possession of his card and was reaching over to collect his money when . . . whoosh!

The male behind him grabbed hold of his back pockets and promptly pulled his jeans down to his ankles.

In an instant, his immediate reaction was to crouch down, grab hold of his jeans to pull them back up, at which point the male culprit behind him calmly reached over, took the £100 cash from the dispenser and ran off.

Totally embarrassed and still trying to adjust his jeans, by the time he realised what had happened, the suspect male had disappeared down the nearest lane, out of sight!

Not wanting to report the incident due to the embarrassment he had suffered, he discreetly informed a few of his colleagues . . . Who in turn, discreetly told me . . . And you!

Semper Vigilo

• • •

Big Hugh Rankin was a crew member of the *Semper Vigilo* police boat. One day they had all enjoyed a lengthy liquid lunch, after which Hugh asked the Sergeant, George Ewart, 'Here, George, why do scuba divers always fall backwards off their boats into the water?'

To which George replied, 'Simple, Hughie! If they were to fall forwards, they'd still be in the fuckin' boat! Wouldn't they?'

Post Office Pusher

. . .

It was the usual Wednesday afternoon for me as I collected wee Flora, my elderly mother, and took her for some lunch prior to doing a bit of household shopping.

En route, I stopped off at the post office to collect her pension money and pay a few of her bills.

As I stood in the queue behind what I can only describe as two absolute cretins, I couldn't help but listen in on their conversation. Particularly as they weren't exactly whispering!

'Ah rattled two bottles o' Buckie last night masel', and I don't even have a hangover . . . not one bit! Wicked or whit?'

'Totally amazing, man. You're a star!' replied the younger one, appearing in awe of this great feat.

He maybe didn't have a hangover, but his breath smelled strongly of a dog's toley . . . And he thought it was pork and herb links he was eating for dinner!

That's a woman for you – take a wee bit too much drink and they take advantage by feeding you any old thing! My own personal weakness is Pedigree Chum and mashed potatoes. Don't laugh, I'm serious. Try some!

Anyways, he continued bragging to the young guy.

'That's fuck all, man. Got stopped wi' two big pandas in a paddy wagon the day. A thought tae masel', 'Uh! Uh! Jamesy boy, you better play it cool here and act neutral.'

'Ye mean natural!' said the young guy, correcting him.

'Same thing, big man!' Jamesy responded. 'The filth walked right up tae my windae and asked me a couple o' easy ones, then he rapidly backed aff and nearly got hit by another motor. Next thing ah know, they're intae their paddy wagon and driving aff up the road. Nae explanation why! Stupit buggers didnae even smell the Buckie aff my breath.

'Ah genuinely thought ah was a certainty tae be spending the next few days in C Block, man, it was pure mental! Know?'

They couldn't smell the Buckie off his breath because it was masked with another smell, as in doggie doo-doo, or maybe a soggy chapatti from the wean's nappy!

Mind you, some o' that stuff that gets dumped in a newborn's nappy could easily be mistaken for a Chic Murray, especially that creamy korma stuff.

'Whit is that smell, man?' asked the young guy.

'Is it that bad?' Jamesy asked, slightly concerned.

'Totally, man. It's bowfin! Totally bowfin!'

They both stood in silence for a few moments, with the Buckie drinker Jamesy cupping his hand and breathing into it then trying to smell it at the same time. All very discreetly, of course, and totally unseen by everybody . . . Except for every one of the thirteen or fourteen customers standing in the post office queue.

Suddenly, he thrust his other hand up to the young guy's face. 'Here, smell that, big man. Whit do you think that is?'

The young guy sniffed his hand, pulled his head back and said, 'The haun ye wiped yer big jazz drum with!'

Jamesy looked down at his hand, then said, 'Sorry, big man, wrang haun, smell this one!'

He held up his other hand and presented it in front of his face.

'Skunk?' responded the younger one.

Jamesy nodded his head. 'Correcto! Only the best! I'm growing it masel'!'

'How many plants have ye got?' he asked.

'Sixteen! Ah had twenty-two, but I couldnae wait for it tae grow, had to try some o' it, so I rolled a few joints . . . Even smoked the stock. I'm just finished watering them there the noo afore ah came here.'

'Sixteen skunk plants? You're a right wee Howard Marks. Growing your own dope in your own wee Mosspark plantation!'

'That's me by the way, an' know whit? They're growing like fucking weeds man, they're massive!'

They both looked at each other and as the penny dropped they both laughed out loud.

'They're growing like weeds – that's a good yin, Jamesy!'

Jamesy then looked around at me standing behind him and slowly stopped laughing, then, turning to face the young guy, he said, 'Turn it down a bit big man. Don't tell everybody in Glesca!' Then he muttered in a loud whisper, 'The big man behind us just might be the filth, so keep it down tae a Hampden roar. By the way, I just might be looking for a business partner, somebody like yourself wi' a few bob behind them.' He then nodded, tapped his nose and winked his eye. 'There could be an opening for you!'

'Let me weigh that up, the head gardener in the Mosspark High Flats Garden Centre, against an offer of a steady job in Ronald MacDonald's cultivating Big Macs and quarter pounders . . . Big decision. A career-changing decision there. I'm afraid I'm gonnae need a bit o' time to think about it!'

'Not a problem, big man, not a problem. Take your time. You'll always get me most days hanging about the Morrisons cafeteria. Spreading the word and taking advanced orders for the big harvesting day.'

'I'd have thought you would be more at home hanging about the organic salad section with the parsley, mint and coriander,' said the young bloke.

Just at that the post office teller interrupted them. 'Next!'

'That's you, Jamesy. It's your turn tae flash your cash card!'

Jamesy moved forward to the counter to be served. After he was finished and about to leave, the younger bloke remarked subtly, 'Is that you away back up to the Beechgrove Gardens to do a wee bit o' weeding then, Mr Nice?'

'You've got tae, man. There's money tae be made, got tae check on my future!' he replied seriously. 'It only takes one o' yon leaves tae touch the heat lamps and – puff – it could all go up in smoke!'

This remark prompted another outburst of impromptu laughter.

'See ye later, Jamesy boy!'

Pole Vaulter

· · ·

A young promoted uniform police sergeant was transferred to 'A' Division in the city centre of Glasgow.

It was nearing the end of his night shift one day as he walked along St Enoch Square, enjoying the quiet and peaceful silence of an early morning stroll, minus the shoppers.

Suddenly, the police Land Rover 'tractor', which could reach 0–60 mph in twelve minutes, flat out, going downhill with a strong following wind, and fitted with go-faster radial tyres, could be heard screeching its way down nearby Union Street as it pursued a stolen car with three male occupants.

As the police Land Rover gave chase, details of the suspects were broadcast over the radio, with a request for assistance.

Just when it turned into the St Enoch Square, one of the front wheels came off the stolen car and it came to a sudden stop, whereby all the neds bailed out, running off in different directions.

Being present within the square, the young sergeant gave chase and apprehended one of the culprits outside the old *Daily Record* offices, whereby he hand-cuffed the ned to a nearby lamp-post and informed the staff to watch him, while he continued with the search for the others.

After a short search came up with no trace of the others involved, the crew from the Land Rover met up with the young sergeant and conveyed him back to the locus where he stated he had restrained one of the accused, hand-cuffed to a lamp-post.

However, during the sergeant's absence, the accused had apparently scaled the tall swan-neck lamp-post like a monkey up a coconut tree, and slipped the cuffs over the top, before sliding back down to the pavement and running off, along with the police-issue hand-cuffs, never to be seen again.

Number-One Idiot

. . .

This is a brief but true scenario from a medical student who is currently working a shift rotation system in the toxicology department at the poison control centre.

Today, a woman called in very upset because she discovered her little daughter was eating live ants.

The student quickly reassured her that the ants she had swallowed were not harmful and there would be no need to bring her daughter into the A & E department of the hospital.

She breathed a huge sigh of relief on hearing this and at the end of the conversation she just happened to mention to him that she'd given her daughter some ant poison to eat in order to kill the ants she had eaten.

He responded by telling her that she had better bring her young daughter into the emergency room immediately to be treated for the poison that she had fed her.

Here's your sign, momma! Wear it with pride, girl.

Name that Chib?

. . .

A wee Glesca punter travelled down south to watch a rugby match between England and Scotland and was sitting at a bar in the Twickenham area when this huge English guy wearing the English national rugby shirt entered the bar.

As he brushed passed the wee Glesca punter, sitting decked out in his colourful tartan kilt and Saltire shirt, he made an unprovoked attack on him, striking him on the back of the neck, knocking him clean off his bar stool and onto the floor. He then announced to everyone present, 'That's what you call a karate chop from China.' He then walked over and took his seat at a table.

The wee Glesca punter recovered, shook his head, got back up onto his bar stool and carried on drinking his whisky.

A short time later, the same big burly Englishman got up from his seat to go to the bathroom and as he walked past the wee Glesca punter, he hit him on the other side of the neck, again knocking him clean off his bar stool onto the tiled floor.

'That's what you call a judo chop from Japan'! he announced to everyone in the bar, before walking off.

The wee Glesca punter once more picked himself up from the floor, shook his head and, deciding he'd had enough, left the pub.

An hour later he returned to the pub, and seeing that the big burly Englishman was now sitting comfortably on the bar stool he had vacated earlier, he casually walked up behind him and whacked him over the head, knocking him clear off the stool, rendering him unconscious on the floor.

He then turned to the bartender and said, 'When that prick wakens up, tell him that's what you call a fuckin' big metal tyre lever from a Ford Transit van.'

Gorbals Cross!

· · ·

One Saturday morning, during the celebrations of the Orange Parade, I was detailed to perform traffic duties at Gorbals Cross.

As I carried out this duty, I would occasionally stop the flow of all traffic in every direction controlled by the busy junction and shout, 'Okay, pedestrians, cross now.' Then I signalled for them to cross over while the traffic was at a stop, before allowing the vehicular traffic to flow again.

I had carried this out several times, but a little old lady dressed in a tweed coat and head scarf remained standing on the sidewalk looking on.

After a short while I shouted for the umpteenth time, 'Pedestrians cross now!'

Suddenly, this little old lady sauntered over to me and said in a broad Irish accent, 'B'Jesus! Is it not about time ye let some of us Catholics across the bloody road?'

Sex, Glesca Style

...

While on holiday, a wee Glesca ned propositioned the services of a local prostitute from the Mosside area of Manchester.

'How much dae ye charge for an hour, doll?'

'£100!' she replied.

'Can ye dae the Glesca method?' he asked her.

'No!' she replied, shaking her head.

'I'll give ye £200 tae dae it the Glesca method.'

'No way!' she said, unaware of what the Glesca method even was.

'I'll give ye £300!'

'No!' she reiterated. 'Now piss off!'

'Awright, awright. I'll give ye £500 then.'

'No!'

Finally he said, 'Tell ye whit, doll, I'll put ye down for a grand if ye'll dae it the Glesca method?'

She thought for a moment, considering the offer being made, and said to herself, 'Well, Helen, you've been in this game for nearly twenty years, you've slept with just about every weirdo out there and took part in some kinky sessions with punters from all over the world, but you've never been offered this much before! How much different can the Glesca method be?'

'Awright lover boy,' she said aloud, 'You're on . . . £1000 to do it the Glesca method!'

And so they stripped off and did it in every way possible, with some impossible 'XXX' positions thrown in.

Finally, after several hours, they finished. The exhausted prostitute turned to the punter and said, 'Here you, I was expecting something weird, perverted and disgusting, but that was bloody good. So why is it called the Glesca method?'

To which the wee Glesca punter replied, 'Because tae get paid, ye need tae send your invoice tae the Social!'

True Love
· · ·

I was invited to an old colleague's home for dinner one evening, during which I was impressed by the way my old buddy preceded every request to his wife with endearments such as 'darling', 'honey', 'sugar', 'pumpkin', 'sweetheart', 'love', and so on.

They had been married almost sixty years and clearly were still very much in love.

While the wife was in the kitchen, I leaned over to my friend and said, 'I think it's amazing after all these years, you still call your wife those loving names.'

My old colleague hung his head and said, 'I have to tell you the truth, Harry. I forgot what her name was about six years ago, but I'm too frightened to ask her what it is!'

The Untouchables

. . .

As you probably know, the nickname 'The Untouchables' comes from a TV crime series about the great Eliot Ness in Prohibition-era USA.

The City of Glasgow police had its own version of the untouchables, which was a team of 'plain clothes' police officers, formed in the city centre division, as a combative anti-crime unit. The officer selected to be in charge of the unit was a Sergeant Hector Boyce.

Sergeant Boyce was well known for his unique undercover disguises – for example, an old 'Columbo' type trench coat with his police radio receiver taped and concealed on his right shoulder to give the impression of a severely disabled person.

He also had a wire with an ear-phone plug taped to the back of his ear, wore dark glasses and used a white walking stick, giving the impression that he was blind.

This disguise was a far cry from the real Hector Boyce, who was a police cross country runner and champion, all-round athlete and regular competitor at the police athletics club meetings.

Therefore it was no great surprise when, in his disabled disguise, he was targeted by neds to be mugged on several occasions in the busy Glasgow city centre.

What was even more surprising – and extremely hilarious – was the look of horror etched across the faces of offenders when pursued and subsequently arrested by their blind disabled male victim with a noticeable disfigurement protruding from his back.

As a master of disguises, Hector excelled in undercover detection, where the conviction rate of his team was exemplary.

With his superb athleticism, and the support of his back-up team of 'Untouchables', it made them a unique crime squad.

'Glesca's Untouchables!' Will ye no' come back again?

Quick Wit!

• • •

This conversation took place in Glasgow several years ago.

The Mounted Branch had been detailed to perform crowd control during an Old Firm football match.

My friend Dick Bruce was a right patter merchant and on approaching a young, very pretty female police officer sitting astride a seventeen-hand-high chestnut horse, which was becoming quite restless due to the long periods of standing still.

Dick decided to chat up the young policewoman and, as he approached her, he was trying to think of something witty to say, which would engage her in conversation.

'Here, hen! Do you know your big horse is frothing at the mouth?'

The young policewoman rider looked him up and down then replied, 'Listen, pal, if you were between my legs for eight hours a day, believe me, you'd be frothing at the mouth too!'

Spiritual Guidance

• • •

One day while at the Ayr race course, gambling on the horses, my former police colleague big John Paton was having no luck whatsoever, until he noticed an elderly Catholic priest stepping out onto the race track, walking over and blessing the forehead of one of the horses lining up for the next race.

Lo and behold, moments afterwards, the horse – an outside long shot – won the race at a canter.

Before the next race took place, as the horses were lining up, big John watched with interest as again the old priest stepped onto the race track and, when the horses came to the starting gate, made a blessing on the forehead of one of the horses.

John made a quick beeline for a betting window and placed a small bet on the horse. Again, even though it was another long shot, the horse the priest had blessed won the race.

John collected his winnings and anxiously waited to see which of the horses would be blessed by the priest in the next race.

The priest again blessed a totally rank outsider of a horse in the line-up. On seeing his choice, John put a big bet on it, and just like the others before, it won comfortably.

John was ecstatic. He couldn't believe his luck.

As the race meeting continued, the elderly priest kept blessing long-shot horses, and each one he blessed romped away from the other horses to come in first.

By this time, big John had won some serious money and with the last race coming up, he knew his wildest dreams were going to come true, so he quickly headed to the nearest ATM and withdrew all the savings from his account, and waited for the old priest to administer the blessing that would indicate which horse he should bet all his money on.

True to form, the priest stepped onto the track for the last race, walked over and blessed the forehead of an old nag that was showing the longest odds of the entire race meeting.

John watched with interest as the elderly priest took his time in blessing the eyes, ears and legs of the old nag.

At that moment, big John knew he had a sure winner and promptly bet every penny he had withdrawn from his account, along with his previous winnings, on the old nag.

He then took up his position in the stand to watch the race.

John was inconsolable as he watched, disbelieving, as the old nag sauntered up to the finishing line in last position, several furlongs behind the rest of the runners, who by this time were enjoying a leisurely rest in their horse boxes, waiting to be conveyed back home to their stables.

John was in a complete state of shock at this unexpected result and made his way down to the horse enclosure area where the old priest was standing.

John couldn't contain himself. He went over to confront the old priest, demanding some answers.

'Father! What happened? All day long I've watched you bless horses before a race and every one you've blessed has turned out a winner. Then, for some unknown reason, in the very last race of the day, the horse that you picked, and you blessed, just lost by a country mile! Now, thanks to you, I've lost all my winnings and every single penny of my life savings.'

The old priest nodded his head sympathetically at John and asked, 'Are you a protestant, by any chance?'

'Yes I'm a protestant! But what has my religion got to do with it?' asked John.

'It has an awful lot to do with it,' replied the priest. 'You see, son, the problem with all you protestants is you don't know the difference between a simple religious blessing and the administering of the last rites!'

Choke!

...

In the early days, prior to the more advanced technology that we have today, we of the older generation used to have motor cars with a manual pull-out choke lever on the dashboard, to assist with starting your car's engine in cold weather.

A choke basically pumped more fuel through the system, after which, once the engine started, you gradually pushed the lever back in to close it, allowing the engine to run normally.

Bill Brydon, a former colleague who worked as a mechanic in the police garage, related a story to me about one of the few policewomen supervisors, who personally called at the garage to collect a panda car, which had been in for repair.

She started the car up and promptly left the garage, only to call the mechanic several hours later, complaining bitterly that the engine was racing excessively fast, coupled with the fact that it was using up exceptional amounts of fuel.

The female supervisor was advised to return the car to the garage for further inspection.

A short time later, she duly arrived outside the garage with the panda car's engine roaring loudly.

As she got out of the driver's seat, she immediately began berating Bill regarding the condition of the car. Bill calmed her down before checking out the car for a fault.

Moments later, Bill had solved the problem of why the engine was racing and using up excessive amounts of fuel.

Apparently, when starting the engine at the garage, she had pulled the choke lever out full, and instead of pushing it back in after she had started the engine, she decided to use the protruding lever to hang her heavy handbag on!

The Showroom

• • •

The divisional commander walked into the police office one morning unaware that his trouser zip was down and his fly area was wide open.

A female inspector approached him and said, 'Excuse me, boss, but when you left your house this morning, did you forget to close your garage door?'

The divisional commander told her 'No', that he knew he'd closed the garage door, and walked off into his office, totally puzzled by her question.

As he finished his morning paperwork, he suddenly noticed his fly was wide open, and promptly zipped it up. He then understood why his assistant had made the remark about his 'garage door'.

He walked out to the front of the office for a cup of coffee and paused at her desk to ask, 'When my garage door was lying open, did you see my Range Rover parked in there?'

The inspector smiled and replied, 'I certainly did not, but I did see an old minivan with two flat tyres!'

Credible Witness

· · ·

My elderly mother went to court as a crown witness and was called to the witness box by the court officer.

The Procurator Fiscal got up from his seat, walked over to the witness box and asked my mother to tell the court her name.

'Flora Morris!' she answered loudly.

'And do you know who I am, Mrs Morris?' he asked.

'Do I know who you are? Of course I know who you are, you're Martin James and I know your mother and father as well.

'I have known you since you were a wee boy living up the next close, and dare I say it, you've turned out to be a real disappointment to your mother. You lie repeatedly, you cheat on your wife and you talk about people behind their backs; you think you're something special, but you're not and you never will be anything other than a jumped-up wee pencil pusher.

'Do I know you? Oh yes, son, I know you very well!' Flora replied.

The Procurator Fiscal was totally stunned by her reaction and, not knowing what else to do, he pointed across at the defence solicitor and said, 'Tell me this, Mrs Morris, do you happen to know Mr Jones sitting opposite?'

'Tommy Jones? Of course I do, I've known him since he was a youngster as well and what a total waste of space he's turned out to be. He's a racist, a bigot, and he's totally bone lazy with a serious drink problem.

'It was that bad, he couldn't hold down a normal relationship with a girl, and broke both his parents' hearts when he was discovered one morning in a hotel bedroom, naked and handcuffed to the bedpost alongside a rent boy, who was snuggled up beside him in the foetal position.

'I feel desperately sorry for his client in the dock.' Then directing her attention to the accused, she said, 'You'd be as well pleading guilty, son, because there's no way that he is going to get you off. You've absolutely no chance!'

The accused looked over at his solicitor for some sort of reassurance. However, on hearing this outburst from my mother, the defence solicitor was in the process of quietly sliding down his chair, trying to disappear out of sight, under the table.

At that, the Sheriff called for order in the court and instructed my mother to take a seat.

He then summoned both the Procurator Fiscal and the defence solicitor to approach the bench, where he whispered to them both, 'If either of you two idiots ask this witness if she knows me, I promise you, your names will be the first on the hangman's list should capital punishment ever be reinstated!'

Jelly Babies

• • •

Retired police officer and cult figure Big Donnie secured a new job doing market research for KY Jelly. While out on his third day in Pollok, he knocked on a door and was greeted by a young attractive lassie, with four small children hanging around at her ankles.

'I'm doing some research for a petroleum jelly company. Can I ask you if you've ever used the product?'

'Oh yes,' she said. 'My husband and I have used it on many occasions.'

'Well if you don't mind my asking,' said Donnie, 'can you tell me what you use it for?'

'Certainly! We always use it when having sex,' she casually replied.

Big Donnie was taken aback with her forthright response. 'Thank you for being so frank, hen, but most people lie to me and say they use it on their child's bicycle chain or on a squeaky gate hinge. But I know for a fact that most people do use it for sex. So I admire you for your honest response, and since you've been so frank so far, can you describe to me how you use it, when having sex?'

This was not exactly a question on his market research question sheet. However, surprisingly the young woman agreed to tell him.

'I don't mind telling you at all. My husband and I put it on the bedroom door-knob and we find it prevents the weans from opening the door and getting in'.

The disappointment on Donnie's face was there for all to see. To tell you the truth, I think he was hoping to hear a more saucy version of events!

As did I when he told me about it later!

Mind the Gap (Bag)

· · ·

While appearing at the Blue Rooms in Liverpool in my one-man show, I wandered out one afternoon and ended up in a lovely little bistro café, where I decided to have my lunch.

I had a small 'Gap'-style shoulder satchel that the missus had bought for me to keep all my personal belongings in. Y'know: wallet, mobile phone, credit cards, and so on. Very 'hip', by the way!

As my lunch was delivered, I was intrigued by the number of signs around the walls emphasising the warning: 'Watch your bags at all times!'

So I did . . . and some bugger stole my dinner!

Bully For You!

...

A farmer in Ayrshire got an unexpected visit from two truck loads of Scottish Power employees who informed him that they were going into one of his fields with their trucks to carry out an inspection of poles carrying their electric power lines.

The weather had been rather inclement at this time of year so Sandy the farmer suggested that if they must carry this out, they inspect their power lines without driving their large, heavy trucks into his field and causing unnecessary damage to his crops. Whereupon one of the Scottish Power representatives immediately produced a clipboard full of official headed paper to show the authority on which they were entitled to enter his field unrestricted.

They promptly walked off, leaving a bewildered Sandy looking on as they continued along the short country road to the field in question, and throwing open the entrance gate they proceeded to drive their heavy vehicles onto his land, cutting it up as they went.

Sandy, not wanting to be so easily outdone, went over to a large shed where he untied his extremely large and intimidating farm bull and led it by the nose ring over to the occupied field, where he promptly released it.

The bull made an aggressive beeline towards the workmen, who were now openly standing beside their trucks, until they saw the fast-approaching out-of-control animal.

As they clambered aboard their trucks, the bull charged around wildly, throwing up divots of earth and crops into the air with its horns, while they looked on fearfully from the safety of their trucks.

While this was taking place, Sandy the farmer stood impassively at the entrance gate and took great delight in shouting over to the workmen, 'Here pal! Why don't you show him yer clipboard full of all your official headed papers and see if he gives a toss!'

As Jim Bowen once said, 'You can't beat a bit of Bully!'

London Train Announcers
• • •

This announcement was a classic!

'Please move all baggage away from the doors.' (Pause.) 'Please move all belongings away from the doors.' (Pause.) 'This is a personal message to Tiger Woods in the blue tracksuit wearing glasses at the rear of the train. Put the Big Mac down, four-eyes, and move your bloody golf clubs away from the train door before I come down there and shove them up your arse sideways!'

Español Por Favor

• • •

While on a recent vacation to Miami, USA, I was sitting enjoying a few drinks with my good friends Dan and Teri Wagnon.

Dan was relating a story about how his wife Teri had been polishing up on her Spanish language while staying at their holiday home in Santa Ponsa, Mallorca.

This particular evening they were out for a meal and the waiter approached their table, greeting them in his broken English.

Teri immediately stopped him and asked him to speak only in Spanish to them, and for her part, she would be ordering her entire evening meal in Spanish.

The waiter nodded in agreement and welcomed her order from the menu to be spoken in his native tongue.

Teri began to order her meal, fluently and effortlessly choosing each course and pronouncing them like a local.

'*Un bottella de casa vino blanco, y gambas y alioli, tortilla Español, pollo con patata fritas, y helado con chocolate. Por favor!*'

Basically, a bottle of house white wine, prawns in garlic, egg and potato omelette, chicken and chips and chocolate ice cream.

After she was finished, the waiter turned his attention to Dan. 'And for you, señor, will you also be ordering your meal in Español?'

Dan looked at the waiter standing there and replied with a confident, '*Si, por favor!*'

After a few moments of perusing the menu, Dan looked up at the waiter who was waiting patiently to hear him fluently ordering in Spanish.

With that, Dan closed the menu, handed it to the waiter, looked him straight in the face and said, '*Dos*!'

One More!

. . .

With my old back injury acting up one night, I shuffled my way slowly into my local ice-cream parlour and pulled myself slowly, agonisingly, up onto a bar stool. After catching my breath, I ordered a chocolate ice-cream surprise.

The waitress looked sympathetically towards me and asked kindly, 'Crushed nuts?'

To which I replied, 'No, hen, arthritis'!

Happy Retirement

· · ·

Tom had been a serving police officer for twenty-five years. Tormented by the everyday stress, he decided to retire from his job and purchase twenty acres of land on the Shetland Isles, as far away from humanity as possible.

A place where he would be lucky to see a postman once a week and store up with groceries once a month. Apart from that, it would be total peace and quiet for the rest of the time.

After eight months of complete and total isolation, he was aroused one morning with a knock at the front door.

He immediately jumped out of bed and answered it, to find a huge, bearded man resembling Grizzly Adams (minus the bear) standing there.

The man stuck out his hand and announced, 'The name's Jack Wilson; I'm your neighbour. I live twelve miles up the road. Just wanted to invite you to a Hogmanay party I'm having at my house on Friday night and thought you might just like to come along and join in. Starts about five o'clock!'

'A party?' Tom responded. 'Definitely! After eight months of living on my own out here with no one to talk to, I'm desperate to meet up with some local folk, that's for sure!'

As Jack was about to leave, he stopped and said, 'Got to warn you. There'll be a lot of drinking.'

'Not a problem, Jack!' Tom replied. 'After serving twenty-five years with the City of Glasgow police, I'm pretty sure I can drink with the best!'

'Probably a lot of cursing and swearing!' added Jack.

'There isn't a swear word or curse that I haven't heard, or used myself,' replied Tom.

Jack was about to leave again, but stopped and added, 'More than likely there's going to be some fighting too!'

'Well, I'm quite a placid guy and get on with most people, so I don't envisage any problem there,' said Tom.

'Probably some wild, rough sexual activity going on too!' Jack added.

'Not a problem for me!' remarked Tom, getting excited at the prospect of meeting up with some 'real' people after all this time.

'As I already said, I've been on my own now for eight months! I'll definitely be there.'

As Jack turned to walk away, Tom called out, 'By the way, Jack, what should I wear to the party?'

To which Jack replied, 'Doesn't really matter, there's only going to be the two of us!'

Y'know, it's at times like this when you really wish you had held on to your old polis baton and handcuffs, just in case things get out of hand!

Gimme Shelter

...

While the missus was in at the dentist, I decided to visit the local charity shops nearby and peruse the books on offer.

I entered the bright-red interior of a Shelter shop, which was presently occupied by several female shoppers looking for the odd bargain.

One customer walked over to the sales assistant and placed on the counter two small vases and a larger vase.

The large vase was priced at £2 but there was no price on the smaller ones accompanying it, so the assistant called over to another woman, who was decorating the window display. 'Sabrina, much is these wee yins?' She held up the vases.

Sabrina looked over at the items being held up and replied, 'Ah'm no' sure, Agnes, ye better ask Martha, she'll know!'

At that, the counter assistant turned her attentions to Martha, on the opposite side of the store, and called out across the floor, 'Martha! Martha! Much is these wee vases?'

Martha looked over at the items referred to and asked, 'Much is the big yin priced at, Agnes?'

'The big yin is priced at £2 but there's nae price on them, and they're much wee'er than the big yin!' Agnes replied. 'So, how much will ah charge this wummin for them?'

'Well ah'm no' very sure, Agnes. Maybe ye better ask Jenny, she'll know best!'

Agnes then turned her attention to Jenny in the back shop.

'Jenny! Jenny!' she called out loudly.

Jenny popped her head out from the back shop. 'Somebody shouting my name?'

'Aye, Jenny, Agnes is shouting for ye,' answered Martha.

'You want me, Agnes?' she called out.

'Aye, Jenny, ah dae. Much is these vases?' she asked.

'Is there no' a price on them, hen?' asked Jenny.

Agnes quickly scrutinised both vases before replying, 'Naw! There's nothing!'

'Whit aboot the big yin? Is it no' priced?' she asked.

'Aye! It's £2 but the wee yins are much wee'er and don't have a price on any o' them,' responded Agnes.

By this time the woman customer was getting slightly frustrated with all that was going on, and I was getting more and more amused by all the chat between each of them.

'Ah'm no' very sure how much. Ye better ask Sabrina, she'll know whit tae charge!'

'Awright, hen!'

Then turning back round to the window dresser, she called out, 'Sabrina!'

Sabrina popped her head around the window, 'What is it, Agnes?'

'Much is these wee yins?' Holding up the vases.

'Ye've already asked me aboot them, Agnes, and ah telt ye ah don't know. Did ye ask Martha like a said?'

'Aye!' she replied. 'She didnae have a clue how much tae charge.'

'Whit aboot Jenny then?'

'Jenny didnae know either! She said ask you,' replied Agnes.

'Well, who was it that priced the big yin?' asked Sabrina.

Agnes picked it up and scrutinised it for a few moments, before responding, 'Ah think it wis me!'

'Ye think it wis you? Well how much did ye price the set at?' asked Sabrina.

'£2!' she replied. 'For the big yin and the two wee yins as part o' the set!'

'Well just charge the wummin £2 for the set then!'

'Awright, Sabrina. Ah knew you'd know how much tae charge. Thanks, hen.'

'Nae bother, Agnes, any time!'

At that, she turned around to relay the price to the customer, who by now was so fed up, she was halfway along the road home to Drumchapel on the bus!

Charity shops – totally stress free! Don't you just love them?!

Plane Crash
· · ·

Ireland has suffered its worst air disaster, which occurred earlier this morning when a small two-seater Cessna plane crashed into a local cemetery.

The Irish police, aided by rescue workers, searched the area and have recovered 1826 bodies so far and expect that number to rise even higher as digging continues throughout the night.

Tom, Dick and Harry

· · ·

Tom died in a fire and his body was burned pretty badly.

The investigating detective needed someone to identify the body, so they sent for his two best friends, Dick and Harry.

The three of them had always done everything together and were locally referred to around Easterhouse as the Three Amigos.

Dick arrived first at the Glasgow City mortuary, and when the attendant pulled back the sheet, Dick looked at the body and said, 'Woah! His face is burned up pretty bad. Can you roll him over and let me see the back of him?'

The attendant obliged and rolled him over, whereby Dick looked on and said, 'Nope, that isn't Tom!'

The detective officer thought this was rather strange, so he brought Harry into the room to confirm the identity of the body.

Harry looked at the body lying there on the trolley, nodded his head and said, 'Wow! He's pretty much wasted. Can you roll him over and let me see him from the back?'

The detective nodded and the mortuary attendant rolled him over as requested.

After viewing the body for a few moments, he said, 'No way, man! This isn't Tom!'

The detective was dumfounded by this and asked, 'How can you possibly tell it isn't him from a view of his back?'

Harry replied, 'Well, sir, it was common knowledge that Tom had two assholes.'

'What?' responded the surprised detective officer. 'He had two assholes?'

'That's what I said. I never seen them for myself, but everybody from Easterhouse who knew him would remark when we were out for a walk with him, "There goes Tom with the two assholes!"'

Number-Two Idiot

• • •

Two armed robbers in Manchester entered a record shop and nervously waved their guns in the air.

The first one shouted, 'Nobody make a move or else!'

At that, everybody in the record shop froze on the spot.

When his partner suddenly went forward to empty the till, the startled first robber turned around and shot him.

He doesn't really deserve to have a sign.

Or What?

· · ·

● Imagine the shock my former police colleague received at getting a letter from his doctor intimating that he only had three months to live. Luckily, the letter was not meant for him; it was actually for his son who has the same name and who still lives in the family home.

Lucky white heather or what?

● What's all this mince about some sixty-six-year-old Italian woman being the world's oldest mother? What rubbish! My wee mammy is eighty-four years old and still going strong.

Now beat that Bella baby!

● What is it with those diabetics? One minute they're having a hypo on the floor with a loved one standing over them screaming, 'Quick! Give him some chocolate! Give him some chocolate!' The following day someone offers them a piece of chocolate and quick as a flash they say, 'No thanks, I'm diabetic.'

Totally confusing or what?

● To the thieving bastards who broke into my house and stole my entire DVD collection, with the exception of *Gone in 60 Seconds*, a film starring Nicolas Cage.

I just hope that when the police eventually catch up with you, the sheriff on the bench takes into account your splendid sense of humour and gives you sixty months.

Reasonable, or what?

● How come my local pub landlord won't serve me if I'm drunk, but down at my local McDonalds they continue to serve all those overweight fat bastards with Big Macs?

Is that fair, or what?

The Auld Enemy

...

Donald was nearing retirement from his tenure as the big polisman of the Highlands.

Prior to his parting of the ways from his beat, Donald received the unexpected news that his replacement for the area was to be Nigel, an English police officer with eight years' police service, who was transferring up to the Highlands from the Metropolitan Police.

Donald greeted him on his arrival the first day, and proceeded to guide him around the area, introducing him to the locals, pointing out the areas of concern and the main offences committed, such as poaching, stealing bird eggs, and so on.

However, Donald was finding it hard going, working closely with his English counterpart, who blatantly stated in no uncertain terms that 'he would police the area his own way'.

This remark from Nigel was the last straw, and Donald was not about to argue with his opinion on policing, therefore out of courtesy he refrained from making any more comments.

The following day while out patrolling the area, Donald pulled up to speak with one of the Laird's gamekeepers. Nigel was disinterested in hearing what was being said, and got out from the police Land Rover, went over to a small Highland burn, and, cupping his hand, he scooped up some water to drink. On seeing this, the Laird's game-keeper shouted, 'Ho! Dinnae drink thon watter man, it's fu' o' coo's shite 'n pish!'

Nigel turned to face him and replied, 'My good man, I didn't understand a word that you uttered from your mouth. Could you possibly repeat what you just said, only this time in English?'

Before the gamekeeper could respond, Donald intervened and shouted, 'He said if you cup both your hands together, you'll get more water that way!'

That's About Right!
. . .

During my time as a police recruit, I was asked at my Training School oral exam, 'What would you do if an occasion arose where you had to arrest your own mother?'

To which I replied, 'Call for back-up!'

Medicine Man

...

During my police service, I must have preached a thousand times and more to my own children, children on the street, in schools, and so on: 'Don't take drugs from anyone! You don't know what you're taking! To do so could prove fatal!'

Harsh words indeed, but very true, so it will come as a surprise to you when I tell you about the time my father-in-law arrived at the house for his annual two-week holiday.

While visiting this particular time, he decided to prune, weed, cut grass and give my garden a general tidy-up.

As I was working back-shift at the time, I wasn't going to deter him – in fact, if truth be known, I actually encouraged him.

Nothing got in his way as he grafted nonstop for three days, gathering all the cut grass and weeds into a neat pile at one side.

I was tucking into my lunch before leaving for duty and Hugh joined me for his. During our conversation over lunch, Hugh complained about not sleeping well due to an aching back problem, aggravated while working in the garden.

Having suffered a severe back injury during my police service and prescribed daily medication of DF118, (Dihydrocodeine) tablets, a very strong pain killer, I suggested he try just half of one, to give him some relief from his suffering, and he agreed.

I gave him the half tablet about 12.30pm that afternoon before bidding him farewell and heading off to my work.

Later that night, on my arrival home at 11.30pm, my wife informed me that Hugh had gone to bed shortly after I left for work, fell into a deep sleep and didn't even get up for his tea.

'I looked in on him about an hour ago and he's still sparkled!' she added. 'Totally out of it.'

'Oh well, he must have been needing it!' I said, satisfied with my prescribed action.

After a mug of tea and a slice of toast, I retired to bed.

The following morning, I was awakened by the kids laughing and giggling, so I got out of bed and went to check on them.

There they were, in Hugh's room, playing on the bedroom floor, with Hugh still sound asleep.

He didn't even stir as I manhandled both of them out of his room to allow him to sleep on and have a long lie.

About 11am, I was making a cup of tea, and decided I would check on Hugh and see if he would like a cup, but on entering his bedroom I started to feel a little uneasy, as Hugh still appeared sound asleep and in the same position, twenty-two hours further on.

As I stood over him staring at his face, I suddenly got the impression that he wasn't breathing.

'Shit!' I blurted out in shock, before bending over him for a closer look at his breathing . . . Nothing!

I stood staring at him for a few moments, just in case he was holding his breath for a laugh, but no. He didn't appear to be breathing. 'He's dead!' I immediately thought.

'Shit! Quick, get me a mirror,' I whispered to my wife out the side of my mouth. 'And keep the weans out there.'

'What for?' asked the missus, a former nurse, with a puzzled expression on her face!

'Just get me a mirror,' I repeated, feeling anxious.

I took the mirror, bent down beside him and put it up to his mouth and waited for his hot breath to cloud the mirror.

And waited! And waited! When suddenly he opened his eyes, looked at his reflection in the mirror against his face and almost had a heart attack on the spot.

'Whit the hell are youse two daying? Ye could have killed me there, ye gave me such a fright!'

Little did he know, that was what I thought too!

'Eh, I'm making some tea, would you like a cup?' I casually asked.

To which he replied, 'How? Is that you finished yer work already? Some shift you dae, I'm telling ye! Ah wish I'd been a polis, bloody part-timers.'

Well! You Did Ask!

• • •

The Community Involvement branch of Strathclyde Police were doing a 'purge' on schools and pushing home their attempts to maintain a close relationship with all pupils, young and old.

An appointment was made to call at Inveraray primary school in Argyll, with a view to speaking openly with the pupils.

During the talk, being conducted by a male and female police officer, the question was posed to the pupils, 'What was your most embarrassing moment?'

They went around the classroom, hearing various scenarios of what they regarded as their biggest embarrassing moment, eventually arriving at a young boy who was sitting patiently awaiting his turn to speak.

'Okay, what's your name then?' asked the policeman.

'My name is Angus,' he responded.

'Okay, Angus, what was your most embarrassing moment?'

'The day my sister walked into my bedroom and caught me masturbating!' he replied forthrightly.

There was complete silence in the classroom for a few moments. You could hear a pin drop it was so quiet.

The police officers were totally speechless and glanced sideways at each other, trying not to appear shocked, as the majority of the classroom began sniggering at this outrageously rude response by Angus.

Trying to look unperturbed by this statement, the male officer decided to break the silence, and asked the first thing that came into his head. 'So what did you do?'

To which Angus replied, to howls of hysterical laughter from his classmates, 'Ah just shut my door over and finished it off!'

Wet Ones

· · ·

An old man goes into a drugstore to buy some Viagra.

'Can I have six tablets, cut into quarters?'

'I can cut them for you,' said the pharmacist. 'But a quarter tablet will not be enough to give you a full erection.

'Erection! I'm ninety-two-years-of-age,' replied the old man.

'I don't want a bloody erection. I just want it sticking out far enough so I don't piss all over my new slippers.'

Betty and Isa

• • •

Yesterday, I called in at my local Shell garage for some fuel.

After I had topped up my car, I walked in to the shop kiosk to pay and took my place at the rear of the small queue.

There were two elderly women at the front and as they approached the counter, the garage shop assistant greeted them.

'Hi Betty! I see you're back again!'

'Naw, it's no' me, William, it's Isa,' she said.

'What? Have you changed your name then?' he asked.

'Don't be silly, it's Isa here,' she replied.

At that, her small frail elderly friend appeared in view from behind her.

'Her! This is Isa,' she said, introducing her friend. 'She needs a few things . . . Right, Isa, tell William whit ye want!'

Isa looked straight at Betty with a blank look on her face and asked, 'Whit dae ah want?'

Rather than tell her directly, Betty gave her a clue to jog her memory.

'Well, what dae ye want tae drink?'

Quick as a flash Isa blurted out, 'Whisky wi' a dash o' green ginger!'

This prompted some smiles and a few sniggers of laughter from the assembled queue, who could see the two elderly ladies at the front of the counter, via the security television screen above their head.

'Well William disnae sell whisky, so what dae ye want tae drink jist noo?'

She then looked right into Isa's face, nodding her head in a prompting way.

'Ginger?' responded Isa.

'Correct! A bottle of ginger, please, William. Right, Isa, what else dae you want?'

'Ah cannae remember!' she replied.

'Of course ye can. I'll give ye another clue . . . Swine flu'!

'Swine flu?' she repeated.

'Aye! Swine flu. It's all the rage jist noo, never oot the news, remember?' said Betty, nodding her head again.

'Swine flu? Oh, ah remember, wis it pork chops?' she answered.

'Naw, ya silly auld cow.'

'Roast beef then?' she quickly responded, changing her previous answer.

'Naw! It wis hankies. Paper hankies! Dae ye remember noo?'

'Och aye! Ah remember! Gimme paper hankies,' she said.

By this time the queue was almost out the door, and most of us standing in it were now laughing and giggling uncontrollably.

'I've only got the big box of tissues,' William said.

'How much are they?' Betty asked.

'£3.29!' he replied.

'£3.29? That's awfy dear. How much is a toilet roll?' she asked.

'Ninety-nine pence for a pack of two,' replied William.

'Jist gimme them. It's only tae wipe my nose,' she said, prompting even more laughter from the patiently waiting queue.

At that, Betty turned to face the crowd behind them.

'Oh come on, Isa, we're holding up the entire shop here. Jist take that the noo and we'll come back down afterwards when William's not as busy!'

Isa began to fidget about her pockets. 'Oh, bugger it!' she said.

'Whit's up noo?' asked Betty.

'I've came oot the hoose without my purse. We'll need tae come back, son. Nae money!' she said, throwing her arms out to the side.

At that, Betty pulled her to one side and said, 'Sorry about that, William. We'll come back down after. We'll go and get a wee cup of tea!'

'Ah cannae wait!' said William. 'Ah look forward to you coming back. Ye make my day!'

Then Isa blurted out, 'Milk! I've nae milk left for my tea!'

Hustling her to the side Betty said, 'I've got some in the fridge!'

At that, Betty and Isa struggled their way through the shop full of queuing, smiling customers with the threat they would return later with money, after a wee cuppa tea.

That's if auld Isa can remember . . .

Remember whit?

Mistaken Identity

· · ·

A drunk who smelled strongly of stale alcohol sat down on a subway train next to a policeman.

The man's shirt and tie were stained, his face was plastered with red lipstick, and a half-empty bottle of whisky was sticking out of his torn coat pocket. He opened the newspaper he was holding and began reading it.

After a few minutes the man turned to the policeman and asked, 'Excuse me, ossifer, what causes arthuritis?'

The policeman replied, 'Well usually it's associated with loose living, hanging about with cheap, wicked women, drinking too much alcohol, contempt for your fellow man, sleeping around with prostitutes and a lack of proper hygiene.'

The drunk muttered in response. 'Well, I'll be damned!' Then he returned to his newspaper.

The policeman, thinking over what he had just said, nudged the drunk man and apologised.

'I'm very sorry about my outburst. I didn't mean to come on so strong. How long have you suffered from arthritis?'

The drunk looked at the policeman and said, 'I don't have it, ossifer. But I was just reading here that your newly appointed Chief Constable does.'

Get Ahead!

. . .

Two of my colleagues in the Traffic Department working out of Inverness police office, were arranging their gear into the car prior to going out on uniform patrol duty.

All systems go, they climbed into their brand-new police Range Rover and drove off, out onto our streets.

After a few moments of driving along the road, their attention was drawn to several members of the public, waving at them. They naturally assumed the public were showing a friendly approach to them, and decided to reciprocate by portraying a positive image and acknowledging them in a courteous manner.

However, they were soon to become increasingly perplexed at the increasing number of pedestrians and fellow motorists waving to them and pointing at their shiny new Range Rover.

Eventually they stopped at traffic lights, and a pedestrian approached the car and tapped on the passenger window.

As the police officer slowly lowered the electric window, the pedestrian informed him that his uniform police hat was hanging over the roof light of their car.

At that, a very red-faced and embarrassed police officer alighted from the car to retrieve it.

Never mind, guys, at least I didn't identify you like your colleagues wanted me to do.

Mind you, I remember partnering a cop nicknamed 'Zippy', who had just bought an Indian curry for his tea when he was approached by a young, attractive female looking for directions.

He placed the curry on the roof of the car, turned around, gave her the directions and promptly jumped into the car.

I had only driven off a few metres when he remembered about the curry and shouted 'STOP!' Which I did immediately, and watched as his curry shot forward and spilled all over the car's bonnet!

Police Hearing!
. . .

Big Jim McGurk, a police motorcyclist, called to see the police chief medical officer complaining of a hearing problem.

'Can you describe the symptoms to me?' Asked Dr McLay.

To which big Jim replied, 'Aye . . . Homer is a fat lazy bastard wi' a big yellow face and Marge is a skinny burd wi' bright blue hair!'

Police Protection

· · ·

During a high profile G8 security training course being held in The Hague, a Strathclyde police officer dressed in full uniform made his way into a local chemist shop.

Very carefully he opened the breast pocket of his police tunic and took out his official notebook.

Opening it up at the beginning, he removed a neatly folded package, which he then unfolded to reveal a small white square handkerchief, and, slowly unwrapping it, he produced a condom.

As he spread it out on the counter, it was most noticeable that the tattered condom had a number of Elastoplast patches on it.

The chemist looked on, scrutinising the item laid out before him, while glancing a look at the police officer, who then asked, 'How much would you take to repair it?'

'The chemist focused on the tattered condom, shrugged his shoulders, shook his head and said, 'Sixty or seventy cents.'

'Sixty or seventy cents?' the policeman repeated, thinking out loud. 'And how much would it be for a new one?'

'One euro,' replied the chemist.

The policeman painstakingly folded up the tattered condom into the white square handkerchief and placed it between the pages of his official notebook, before replacing it carefully into the breast pocket of his tunic and walking back out of the front door.

Moments later, the chemist heard the front door opening again, followed by a shout for service.

He looked out to see the same police officer standing at the front counter with a grin on his face.

'Can I help you?' asked the chemist.

'Ye sure can!' said the police officer. 'The boys have taken a vote and decided – we're just going to buy a new one.'

Donnie Tales
• • •

When we were police probationers, one of the students on my course was telling me that he was sleeping with his girlfriend and her twin.

I asked, 'How do tell them apart?'

He replied that it was very easy: her brother's got a moustache!

Having a Bad Day

...

If you think you are having a bad day, let this cheer you up.

A wee Glesca woman came home from work to find her policeman husband in the kitchen twitching away frantically, with some kind of wiring going from his waist towards the electric kettle on the worktop.

She took immediate emergency action to free him from the deadly current, by whacking him with his police-issue PR24 truncheon, thereby breaking his arm in two places.

Up to that moment, he had been happily practising his John Travolta disco dance moves, while listening to his iPod.

STILL think youre having a bad day?

Two animal rights protesters were demonstrating with banners at the cruelty of sending pigs to an abattoir in Paisley, when suddenly, all 200 pigs being delivered broke free and escaped through a broken fence, stampeding madly.

Alas, the two hapless animal rights protesters were directly in their way and, as a result, were trampled to death by the very pigs they were protesting about.

STILL having a bad day? Well this last one is a complete classic.

An Iraqi terrorist, Khay Rahnajet, didn't pay enough postage on a letter bomb he was sending to a local police station.

Subsequently, it came back to him with the words 'return to sender' stamped on it.

Forgetting it was the bomb he had sent, he promptly opened it up, and surprise, surprise, he was blown to bits.

Which reminds me of a story about a Suicide Bomb Instructor who stood in front of his class of potential suicide bombers and, as he was about to detonate the explosives he was wearing, he said, 'Pay attention, 'cause I'm only going to show you this once!'

There now, feeling better?

That Was the Start
· · ·

When I arrived home last night from a police outing at the golf with the rest of my shift, my wife demanded that I take her some place expensive. So I took her to a petrol station and filled up the car.

The Bunny Boiler

· · ·

Sergeant Hector was the shift duty officer in charge of the Pollok police office in Glasgow.

On his weekend off, along with the wife and kids, he took off to his family country cottage in a small village just outside Campbeltown, accompanied by the latest family pet, an unusual white-coloured Cocker Spaniel dog.

On their arrival at the cottage, with it being a sunny day, the dog's collar with fancy name tag was removed in order to provide it with its first pet bath.

After the ceremonial first bath, which involved lots of pampering and towel drying, it was tethered outside in the sun to dry off.

A short time later, the youngest daughter went outside to give it some food and discovered that it had chewed its way through the lead and escaped through a hole in the garden fence.

Being quite near to the main road, a search was made to try and locate it, but no trace was found of the pet.

Later that evening, having exhausted their search, Hector made his way to the local pub for a much needed pint.

It was while standing at the bar enjoying his pint that he overheard a drunken local relating a story from earlier that day, of how on his way home from the pub earlier that afternoon, he had come across a giant white rabbit in the middle of the road, sitting on its hind legs with its paws and tail wagging.

Without going into too much more detail, suffice to say, he captured it and took it home with him.

On hearing this news, big Hector promptly informed him that it was in fact a dog, not a rabbit, and that they had been searching for it all afternoon.

Where was it now?

The drunken local informed Hector, that the big rabbit, as he had described it, was now in a large cooking pot, where he had boiled it alongside various vegetables.

Big Hector couldn't listen to any more of the drunken local's raving. He immediately grabbed hold of him by the scruff of the neck and put a death grip on him, while at the same time informing him that he was a police sergeant from Glasgow.

The rest of the pub patrons intervened to separate both men, as Hector proceeded to choke him.

As they struggled to hold him down, the irate Hector could be heard shouting at the top of his voice, 'Away, ya drunken auld bastard, you've eaten ma wean's wee pet dug!'

Suddenly the door to the pub was thrown open and in came Hector's wife all excited, accompanied by his weans, leading the pet Cocker Spaniel on a rope.

They all focussed on Hector being restrained by half the pub locals, as one of his weans called out, 'We've found her, Daddy!'

After a short while peace was restored and after a bit of heavy grovelling by Hector, a drink settlement was made, as everyone in the pub ordered large whiskies at Hector's expense.

Where had the dog been, I hear you ask?

It appears that the lost pet dog had been found by the local policeman after he came across it on the hills chasing after real bunnies, 'Born Free' style.

Silence That Man!

· · ·

Alistair Petrie was a very straight, ex-military-type individual, and being ex-army, he was always immaculately turned out in his police uniform.

He was bald-headed as a personal preference, with a pencil-thin moustache, neatly trimmed without a hair out of place.

Alistair was a senior cop with years of experience and would regularly be accompanied by a young recruit, with whom he would march up and down the empty sheds of the Kingston Docks, executing every drill movement possible, every instruction called out by himself – with no swearing, as would have been expected from a Sergeant Major!

One particular evening, Alistair had conveyed a prisoner to the Gorbals Police Office.

While awaiting his turn, in a queue of prisoners all waiting to be charged, Alistair's prisoner was disturbing the others by continually shouting, swearing and bemoaning his arrest.

As the charge bar area was very busy at this time, the Duty Officer was becoming exasperated and called out, 'Silence that man!'

Alistair, always one to obey an order, shouted back, ' Yes sir!' Then drew his wooden baton and promptly struck his prisoner across the head, knocking him unconscious!

The other prisoners looking on were speechless. You could hear a pin drop.

As for the explanation as to the injuries to his prisoner? Alastair reported that 'Obviously he had too much to drink, fell in the street, and was subsequently found lying there in that condition by myself.'

Problem solved, prompting a thank-you letter from the prisoner's immediate family for being so caring in looking after him.

Question & Answer

· · ·

What has a hundred legs and three teeth?

A methadone queue.

Judge Judy

· · ·

Judge Judy asked a prostitute, 'So when did you realise you were raped?'

The prostitute, wiping away her tears, said, 'When his cheque bounced!'

Flying

...

Back in the 60s, a police casualty surgeon was asked to accompany an elderly sergeant, renowned for having a reputation as a joker.

It was late in the evening and very little was happening, so they decided to park near the 'Whirlies' roundabout in East Kilbride and take observations.

They had only been there a few minutes when from the town centre direction appeared a small, two-seater sports car with fancy wire spoke wheels, racing towards the roundabout.

The elderly sergeant immediately turned to the police doctor and said, 'I think we might require your services very shortly!'

The words had hardly left his lips when the car ploughed straight into the roundabout at high speed, causing the bodywork to detach from the chassis on impact. It then continued to career up the grass slope, coming to rest in the centre of the roundabout.

The elderly sergeant heaved a heavy sigh, stepped out of the police car, put on his hat and walked slowly towards what was left of the sports car.

The driver was still seated in the driving seat, which was wedged at an awkward angle. Apart from appearing slightly dazed, the driver looked okay.

'Are you all right there, son?' the sergeant asked.

The driver nodded his head and replied, 'Yes.'

'Okay then, driving licence?' said the sergeant.

On checking it, the sergeant noted that the licence was issued by the RAF and the driver held the rank of pilot officer.

The elderly sergeant couldn't resist it, as he looked at the driver and with a wry smile, and said, 'Okay, Pilot Officer, what's it to be? Reckless driving, or dangerously low flying without wings?'

Depressed

...

I was so depressed last night, I rang *Lifeline* and got through to a call centre in Afghanistan, so I told the operator I was deeply depressed and feeling suicidal.

The guy got all excited and asked if I could drive a truck.

Shopping at Morrisons

. . .

Yesterday I was at my local Morrisons store buying a large bag of Iams dog biscuits for my wee dog, Jock, the wonder dog. I was standing in the checkout line when the woman behind me asked if I actually had a dog.

What did she think I had, a horse? So, being a retired polis and with little to do these days but practise my sense of humour, I reacted on impulse and replied, 'No, I don't have a dog, but I am starting my Iams Diet again.'

I added that I probably shouldn't, because I'd ended up in the hospital the last time, having lost four stones before collapsing and waking up in an intensive-care unit with tubes and wires coming out of every orifice, coupled with drips in both arms.

I told her that it was essentially a perfect diet and that you fill your trouser pockets with Iams nuggets and simply eat one or two every time you feel hungry. The food is nutritionally complete, so it works well, and therefore I was going to give it another try.

At this point, I have to mention that practically everyone in the checkout queue was now totally engrossed with my fascinating story about my dog biscuits.

However, horrified at the thought, the woman asked if I had ended up in intensive care because the dog food had poisoned me.

'Absolutely not!' I responded. 'It was because I stepped off the footpath onto the roadway to sniff a Golden Retriever's bum, and was struck by an oncoming car.'

I thought the man behind her in the queue was going to have a massive heart attack, he was laughing so hard.

As a result, Morrisons won't let me shop there any more. So as a warning to you all, think before you ask us retired polis daft questions, because we have all the time in the world to think up some crazy stories to shock you with.

Bloody Cheek

· · ·

One night, while alone in the house with my missus, I thought I was being funny and said to her, 'Maybe we should start washing your clothes in that Slim Fast. It would take a few inches off your waist!'

My wife was not one bit amused, and decided that she simply couldn't let such a comment like that go without getting back at me.

The very next morning I took a pair of underpants out of my drawer. 'What the hell is this?' I said to myself, as a little puff of dust cloud appeared when I shook them out.

'Ho, Maz!' I shouted into the bathroom. 'Why did you put talcum powder into the crotch of my underpants?'

She shouted back, 'It's not talcum powder ... it's bloody Miracle Grow!'

Car Boot Sale

...

One of my favourite pastimes is walking around a car boot sale. In fact, I'll go as far to say that I suffer withdrawal symptoms if I miss a Saturday morning rummage at a stall.

Last week, I was spreading my wealth on a visit to my local car boot venue when I was drawn to a small ornate-looking vase. I picked it up for closer inspection, before enquiring, 'How much is this?'

The woman looked over at the item I was holding, screwed her eyes up to see it better, then turned to her male partner who was accompanying her and said, 'Ya rotten big bastard! Ah suppose this is your idea of a joke?'

At that, she leaned over and politely grabbed it out of my hand. 'You'll pay for this, ya big diddy. You've taken it too far this time.'

'Whit? Whit's yer problem?' he asked her, with a smirk on his face.

'This!' she replied, holding up the item.

'Oh that? It was a wee accident!' he responded. It must have fell in the box by mistake.'

'Fell in the box by mistake, my arse . . . You know fine well that's my mammy's ashes in there. Ye're a rotten big bastard, but don't worry, you'll be sorry.'

All the while I stood there soaking up their argumentative conversation as he continued to try and explain away his actions.

'Let's face it, when she was alive, she widnae let us go anywhere oorsel', she always had tae come wi' us, so ah thought ah'd bring her alang tae her first car boot sale!' he replied. 'Ah wisnae gonnae really sell her. It was just a wee day out for her. That was a'!'

'Well ye've went too far this time. Just wait, I'll get ye back for this. See your faither's ashes, you'll be getting spoonfuls of him in yer tea, yer porridge, yer mince . . . You watch me, ye'll be eating him a bit at a time and ye'll no' be any the wiser! And see whit ye don't eat, it'll be getting scattered into the cat's box. I'm gonnae make you and him suffer for this.'

She then turned around to face me and blurted out indignantly, 'She isnae for sale at any price, I'm keeping her!'

Car boot sales – sometimes, ye just don't know what ye're buying!

Training School

· · ·

The Tulliallan Drill Sergeant noticed a new police recruit walking across his parade square and bawled at him, 'Here you! Get your ass over here now!'

The new recruit tentatively made his way over to him.

'What's your name?' he screamed at him.

'George!' the new recruit replied.

'Listen here, I don't know what kind of bleeding heart, pansy potter bullshit they're teaching you lot at the new Jackton police college, but up here, we don't refer to anyone by their first name,' the sergeant scowled. 'It leads to familiarity, and familiarity breeds contempt and a total breakdown in authority. Therefore, I refer to all new recruits by their surnames only, such as Morris, Clark, Bell. As for me, I don't want you to refer to me as sir, sarge, boss or any other alias; I'm to be addressed as sergeant. Do I make myself absolutely clear?'

The new recruit responded nervously. 'Yes, Sergeant!'

'Thank you! And now we've got that straight, what's your surname?'

The new recruit heaved a huge sigh, visibly gulped and said, 'Darling! My name is George Darling.'

The drill sergeant paused for a few moments, took a deep breath then said, 'Right! Okay, George, here's what I want you to do . . .'

Do What She Says!

...

A young opportunist ned housebreaker was wandering around a housing estate looking for his next property with an obvious opening for him to exploit, when he noticed a note pinned to the front door.

He casually entered through the front gate and walked up to the door where he removed the note, which was addressed to 'The Repairman', and contained the following information:

'Keys are under the door mat. Faulty dishwasher in the kitchen, off to the right as you enter the house. After you have repaired it, leave your invoice on the work top and I'll send you off a cheque for the amount.

'Oh, by the way, don't worry about my dog Spud. He won't bother with you. However, whatever you do, do NOT, under any circumstances, talk to my parrot! I must stress that you totally ignore my parrot and do not talk to him!'

Having read her written instructions to the repairman, the young ned located the key from under the mat and opened the front door of the house and entered, where he encountered the biggest, meanest looking dog he had ever seen. But, just as she had said in her note, the dog just lay there on the carpet watching the young ned go about his work of emptying drawers and cupboards looking for items of value to steal.

The parrot, however, drove him nuts the whole time he was doing this with its incessant squawking, swearing and continual offensive name calling.

Finally the young ned couldn't stand it any longer and yelled, 'Shut it, ya stupid, ugly bird or, I'll stick ye in the oven!' To which the parrot responded: 'GET HIM SPUD!' Y'know, sometimes you should listen to what women have to say!

Dose of Claim-itis!

. . .

You'll have seen the adverts on the television, or maybe heard them on the radio, regarding Health and Safety issues, with companies wishing to represent you in trying to get you a claim for compensation, if you have suffered an injury in the work place, or while out driving your car.

Well this is the Glesca version of the same advertisement.

Have you been injured at work lately?

Had a car accident while out driving?

Slipped on a wet floor in the work place?

Or tripped and fell injuring yourself on an uneven surface?

If so . . .

You're probably just a clumsy auld bastard!

Rambo Granny!

. . .

The person who told me about this gun-toting grand-mother alleges it's true, so I'm going to relate it to you.

Apparently an elderly granny, on hearing that two thugs had violently raped her sixteen-year-old granddaughter, took it upon herself to seek revenge by tracing the where-abouts of the unsuspecting accused rapists and shooting off their testicles. Afterwards, she drove to the nearest police station, placed her firearm on the sergeant's desk and informed him very calmly, 'Those bastards who raped my granddaughter will never rape another girl, that's for sure!'

The police report stated that the previously convicted rapist and armed robber David Murphy had lost his penis and both testicles when the outraged gun-toting granny opened fire on him with a .44 Magnum pistol in the hotel room where he and former prison cell mate Sidney Lomas were hiding out.

The avenging granny had also blasted Lomas's testicles to kingdom come, but, unfortunately, a team of doctors managed to save his mangled penis.

A police spokesman was quoted as saying, 'Lomas may not have lost his manhood, but the doctor I spoke with said he won't be using it the way he used to!'

Detective John Dodds told reporters, 'Both the accused are in a pretty bad condition, but are only too happy to be alive after what they've been through.'

'Rambo Granny', as she is now being referred to by the public, took the drastic action after her granddaughter had been carjacked and raped by the knife-wielding accused males in broad daylight, only minutes from a busy shopping mall.

'When I saw the look on my granddaughter's face that night in the hospital, I decided to go out and get those bastards myself,' the retired library assistant recalled. 'I wasn't scared of them, because I had my gun with me and I've been shooting guns all my life.

'So, using the police artist's sketch of the suspects involved and my granddaughter's description, I spent the next seven days prowling the wino-infested neighbourhood where the crime took place till I spotted them entering their hotel. I knew it was them the minute I saw them. So I went into the hotel, found their room and knocked on the door. When the big one opened the door, I shot him right between the legs. Then I casually walked inside and shot the other bastard as he cowardly backed up pleading for mercy.

'When I'd finished with him, I went down to the local police station and handed myself in.'

Now, the problem is, the baffled lawmen are trying to figure out exactly what to do with their vigilante granny!

'What this woman has done was wrong, and she broke the law, but it is difficult to throw an eighty-one-year-old woman into prison,' said a police spokesman, before adding, 'Especially when there are several thousand people in the area wanting to nominate her for the next mayor of the city!'

You don't know what to do with her?

Well why not deport her to the UK? We'll give her a job to do!'

Daktari

· · ·

A retired sea captain living in the King's Park area of Glasgow had a pet monkey, which he kept in his house.

One particular day, the captain had gone out and forgotten to close his back door, as a result of which his pet monkey managed to escape from the house.

A concerned neighbour contacted the police and Sergeant Sinton duly arrived, accompanied by several other officers, intent on capturing the monkey, which was presently having a field day cavorting about the neighbourhood gardens, swinging on trees and bushes, while evading all attempts to capture it.

Sergeant Sinton deployed his officers tactfully around the nearby gardens and managed to corner the animal.

With the monkey now surrounded by his officers, the sergeant decided to make a dive and grab it.

As he poised in readiness to carry out this manoeuvre, he made his move, swooping down on the monkey like an Olympic diver off the top board.

Unfortunately for him, within a split second of him doing so, the monkey nimbly leapt to the side, leaving the sergeant grasping at thin air and coming to rest in a muddy puddle of rain water.

The monkey shot a look of disdain at the bedraggled police sergeant getting up from the puddle, before it casually walked over and re-entered the house via the back door.

Unfortunately, that was not the end of the incident, for with each passing day the story 'grew legs' and became exaggerated.

Thereafter, for the rest of his police service, Sergeant Sinton was given the nickname of 'Daktari' after a popular African wildlife TV drama from the 60s.

Anniversary
• • •

I asked my missus last night, 'Where do you want to go for our anniversary, darling?'

It warmed my heart to see her face light up in sweet appreciation as she pondered for a few moments before responding, 'Somewhere that I haven't been in a long time!'

So I immediately suggested, 'How about the kitchen?'

Where Are You?

· · ·

Last week I had to go to Spain on a promotional tour for my new children books.

As my missus was not accompanying me, she offered to drop me off at the car park in front of the airport in plenty of time to catch my Ryanair flight to Murcia.

A week later, I was boarding my flight home and prior to take off, I texted my wife to let her know I would be on time.

Having boarded the plane, I managed to secure a seat, right at the front, next to the main exit door.

After a very uneventful flight, during which I slept most of the way, we arrived safely at Prestwick Airport.

With just a small shoulder bag in the overhead locker, as soon as the exit door was opened, I quickly collected it and was first off down the stairs and onto the tarmac.

I was first through the Customs / Passport section, and I was even first through the empty baggage hall.

I was way out in front, having left the rest of my fellow passengers behind in my path.

So slick was my exit from the plane, I was even first through the airport arrival lounge and out the front doors of the terminal building heading for the car park in first position.

I quickly rang my missus. 'That's me landed, hen, where are you?'

'I'm in the garage around the corner, be with you in a few minutes.'

I stood there in anticipation, eager to see her after my week-long tour.

Suddenly, my mobile rang and my missus asked, 'Where are you, Harry?'

'I'm right outside the front door of the airport,' I replied.

'Okay!' she said. 'I'll come back round. Don't move!'

Several minutes passed, as I stood there watching all the other passengers that I had left behind appear out the front doors and head off in their cars.

Then the phone rang again and I answered. 'Where are you now?' my missus asked.

'I'm not anywhere! I'm still standing in the car park, in the same place where you dropped me off!' I responded.

'Well go to the big Budget Car Hire sign,' she said. 'I'll get you there.' At that she hung up.

After a few minutes of looking around, trying to locate a 'big Budget Car Hire sign', I was compelled to call my missus back to ask her, 'Darling! What airport are you at?'

'Glasgow of course! Where do you think I am?' she replied promptly and rather indignantly.

Then there was a long pause before it dawned on her and she replied, 'Oops! You're in Prestwick, aren't you?'

'Yep!' I replied. 'And I'm standing in the exact same spot you dropped me off at. Remember now?'

There was another long silence, followed by, 'Wait for me, I'll be right there!'

Hookers Feel the Pinch!

. . .

Now that the credit crunch is getting a real grip, no one is escaping it!

Even the price of sex in the red light area of Glasgow has now fallen for the seventh month in a row, giving rise to several pairs of sexy legs being covered up, closed up and moved away to pastures new to try and find work.

One prostitute has told a member of the Strathclyde Police Vice Squad that she is now charging her lowest prices for sex in twenty-five years.

The price of a kiss is now only a pound, with a BOGOF offer, and a fifteen-minute snog is as low as £2.50.

Other reductions being introduced include a grope at her bum for a mere £3, while a feel at a breast is only £3.50, or two for a fiver!

Sabrina is a regular prostitute who has been working the area for many years now, and who has experienced the highs as well as the lows.

'Ah'm having tae introduce a lunchtime "Credit Crunch Special" tae my punters, incorporating many of my favourite sexual positions,' she said. 'That Cynthia Payne had the right idea wi' the luncheon vouchers!'

When asked what exactly her lunchtime 'Credit Crunch Special' involved, Sabrina replied, 'Jist like the Griffin Pub aroun' the corner, I'm offering a starter, a main course and a wee trifle afore ye go for a fiver! Noo that's cheap. Here, take one of my leaflets with the new price list.'

At that she handed over a colourful photograph flyer of

herself (twenty years younger, of course) detailing in her own descriptive words the services she provides, and her lowest 'bottom' discount prices.

There was even a highlighted special offer for a Monday night, where it was two for the price of one. Apparently this offer was proving to be a popular choice with the students at a nearby university, after which many of them took handfuls of her flyers away to distribute around the campus.

The drop in paying customers in the area is also a big worry for Strathclyde Police who have been forced to relocate several members of the highly popular Vice Squad, assigning them to other duties of similar importance such as robberies, thefts, muggings and murders.

This lack of interest in the sexual trade has seen many companies in the area suffer, with private car parks closing their doors early.

Even the famous male stripper group the Chippendales have had to introduce cut-backs, and are now a duo going by the name of Chip 'n' Dale, as well as their main rival and competitor, the 'Dream Boy'.

We left Sabrina to have the last word and sum up this crisis. Over to you, Sabrina:

'Ah wis jist saying tae yer cameraman, at one point ah wis that busy, my knickers were up and doon more often than an elevator at the Hilton. My business was booming, ah couldnae keep my legs shut. Only last year, I reckon I had more rides than Frankie Dettori, but nowadays, the only time my legs are open for any length o' time is when I'm walking up the road tae go back home! Mind you, it's good tae get the bed tae masel'!'

Glesca Family Planning

· · ·

After giving birth to their twelfth child, named Princess Crystal Chandelier Larsson O'Neill the eighth, a pair of Glesca sweethearts decided enough was enough!

This came as a result of being unable to afford a bigger bed.

The hubby decided to see his family GP and inform him that he and his missus didn't want to have any more children.

The doctor explained that there was a procedure that could help him with this request, called a vasectomy, and that he could solve his problem, but, unfortunately, the procedure was expensive.

'However!' said the doctor. 'A much cheaper alternative is to go home and get a firework banger, light the blue touch paper, drop it into an empty beer can, then hold the can up close to your ear and count to ten, and then wait.'

The Glesca hubby, in the Charlie Nicholas parlance, said to the doctor, 'I might not be the smartest tottie in the fruit basket, but I cannae see how putting a firework in a beer can, then up next to my ear, is going to help me with my problem.'

'Trust me, I'm a doctor,' responded his GP assuredly.

With these few words of wisdom, the hubby went home, lit a firework banger and dropped it into a beer can.

He then carried out the rest of his GP's instructions to a tee, held the can up to his ear and began to count, 'One, two, three, four, five . . . ' At which point he paused for a moment, placing the beer can with the lit banger between his legs and resumed counting, using his other hand, of course, when . . . 'BANG!'

This procedure is apparently now available on the NHS and has been proven to work, with highly successful results being recorded in Govan, Drumchapel, Garthamlock, Ferguslie Park, Parkhead, Coatbridge, Shettleston and Castlemilk.

Room Service
. . .

A newly promoted assistant chief constable was through in Edinburgh attending a police seminar. He had called ahead and booked hotel accommodation.

Arriving at the hotel he asked the receptionist, 'Is the TV porn channel in my room disabled?'

'No,' she replied. 'It's just a normal adult porn channel.'

I A*** You!
. . .

A man was driving in his newly purchased sports car and testing its performance as he sped along what appeared to be a quiet road, when he suddenly observed a uniformed traffic cop on the footpath with a radar speed gun aimed directly at him, signalling for him to pull over to the side of the road.

The man duly obeyed the signal and pulled into the lay-by at the side of the road, aware that he was being stopped for speeding, totally disgruntled at being caught.

The traffic cop walked up to the driver's side of the car and on reaching the window he said to the man, 'Well sir. I would have thought that with a car like this, you would've wanted to hold onto your driving licence?'

'I do!' replied the man.

The traffic cop then looked around the car, admiring it, and said, 'You must have a right good paying job to own this baby?'

The man replied, 'Actually, I do, I am an anus stretcher.'

'An anus stretcher?' asked the cop. 'What exactly is that?'

'Well, firstly it involves me having to insert two fingers and stretch the anus, working up to two hands then two arms and then I use my arms and my feet and stretch it as wide and as big as I can.'

The cop was amazed. He asked, 'How wide do you stretch to?'

'Usually about six feet!' he replied.

At this point the cop was totally taken in by this explanation and couldn't resist asking, 'So, what do you do once you have a six-foot arsehole?'

To which the man replied, 'Well, we usually issue him with a uniform, give him a radar speed gun and tell him to hide behind a bush on the footpath!'

Police Exams
. . .

An Instructor at Tulliallan Police College reminded the students of the following day's final exam.

'Now listen to me. The adjudicators will not tolerate any excuse for you not being here tomorrow.

'They may consider a nuclear attack or a serious personal injury or illness, they may even consider a death to a member of your immediate family, but that's it, no other excuse whatsoever will be accepted!'

A smart-arsed mature student, 'Winker Watson', seated at the rear of the room, raised his hand and asked, 'What would happen if I came in tomorrow suffering from complete and utter sexual exhaustion?'

The other students in the class tried desperately to stifle their laughter at Winker's remark.

When order was restored, the instructor smiled at the mature student, shook his head and said, 'Well I suppose you'd just have to write with your other hand! Wouldn't you? Wanker.'

An Expert Witness

• • •

I love it when I hear a good court case where a cop has got the upper hand on some smug defence agent. This was one such case.

A young police officer was being cross-examined by a well-known defence lawyer during a robbery trial. This particular lawyer, as per usual, was trying to undermine the credibility of the police officer.

'Officer, can you tell the court, did you see my client fleeing the scene of the crime?'

'No sir, but I did observe a person matching the description of the suspect, running off further along the road,' the cop replied.

'Can you tell the court who provided you with this exact information and description?' asked the lawyer.

'The first police officer who attended at the scene.'

'So it was a fellow police officer who provided you with the description of this suspect. So tell me this, do you trust your fellow officers?'

'Most definitely, sir. I trust them with my life!' he replied

'With your life? Well that's a brave statement, so let me ask you this: Do you have a changing room in the building where you prepare for your daily court duties?' asked the lawyer.

'Yes sir, we do.'

'And do you have a locker in that room?'

'Yes sir, I do,' replied the officer.

'And I presume you have a lock on your locker?' he asked.

'Yes sir, I have a padlock.'

'Well can you explain to the court why someone who has just stated he trusts his fellow officers with his life would find it necessary to padlock his locker, in a room that he shares with these very same officers?' He then sat back in his chair with a smug look on his face, awaiting the young officer's response.

The young cop paused for a few moments, as he looked towards the Procurator Fiscal and then towards the Sheriff on the bench, and asked, 'Do I have to answer m'lord?' he asked the Sheriff.

'Yes, Officer, you do,' he replied.

At this the defence lawyer was overwhelmed with smugness as he looked towards his client and winked his eye.

'Can you repeat the question please?' asked the officer.

'Certainly!' responded the lawyer, getting to his feet. 'I asked you to explain to the court why someone who has just stated he trusts his fellow officers with his very life, would find it necessary to padlock his locker, in a room that he shares with these very same police officers?'

All eyes in the court then focussed on the young police officer, who paused for a moment before responding.

'Well it's like this, sir, I never said I padlocked my locker because of my police colleagues.'

'Oh no! Well please tell this court why is it that you find the need to padlock it then?' the lawyer asked again.

'Well, sir, we share part of the office building with the court complex, and with all due respect, sometimes lawyers, such as yourself, have been known to wander through the changing room into our private locker area to use the toilets.'

The entire courtroom erupted in laughter.

Number-Three Idiot

· · ·

Earlier this year, some Boeing employees on the airfield decided to steal a life raft from one of the 747 aeroplanes they were working on.

They were successful in getting it out of the plane and home.

One day, while out for a sail on the river, they noticed a Coast Guard helicopter coming towards them.

It turned out that the chopper was homing in on the emergency beacon that was activated when they inflated the raft.

Surprise, surprise! They are no longer employed by Boeing.

The Glesca Gangster

. . .

A one-time infamous retired Glesca gangster was invited to a wedding in Manchester.

After one whisky too many at the party, he went outside for a cigarette and walked off without any of his henchmen to accompany him. Before he knew it, he was lost.

Wandering about alone and vulnerable in the Moss Side area, he noticed a gang of young 'hoodies' heading rapidly in his direction with the intention of beating him up and relieving him of all his hard-earned scran, such as his Gucci wallet, Rolex watch, gold rings and Bulgari bracelet.

The old gangster thought, 'Uh-oh! I'm in deep shit now!'

Noticing an old drunken wine drinker lying unconsciously flat out on the ground close by, he immediately settled down beside him, with his back to the approaching gang.

Just as the hoodies were about to attack him, he exclaimed loudly, 'Boy oh boy, you were a tough old bastard. Fifty-four times I had to stab you afore ye stopped wriggling about! I think I'll just shoot the next one and save all my energy!'

Hearing this, the young hoodie gang halted their attack, and a look of fear came over them as they all skulked off in different directions towards the flats.

'Whew!' said the hoodie gang leader, 'That was close! That old bastard might have done a few of us!

Meanwhile, another old wine drinker who had been watching the entire episode from a nearby shop doorway figured he could put this knowledge to good use and trade it for protection from the hoodie gang. So off he went to tell them.

However, the old gangster spotted him heading off after the hoodies and figured that something must be up.

The wine drinker soon met up with the gang leader and told him how he had been conned by the Glesca gangster.

He then struck a deal for himself with the hoodie gang leader for a share of the spoils.

The hoodie gang leader was furious at being made a fool of and said to the wine drinker, 'Right you, come with us and see what's going to happen to that conniving old bastard!

Now, the old Glesca gangster saw the hoodie gang coming towards him along with the wine drinker and thought to himself: 'What am I going to do now?' But instead of trying to outrun them, the old gangster knelt down with his back to his attackers, pretending he hadn't seen them yet, and just when they got close enough to hear him, the old gangster uttered out loud,

'Where's that auld wino diddy? I sent him aff an hour ago tae bring me back some o' they wee hoodie neds tae shoot!'

Moral of this story: Don't mess with old farts. Mature in age and treacherous in their early days, they will always overcome youth and skill!

Bullshit and balls only come with age and experience.

Mini Minors

· · ·

Wednesday was, as per usual, purple rinse day. That's my special day for treating my wee mammy, when we have a spot of lunch before doing the household shopping, then up the road for a cup of tea and a strawberry oyster cake each.

During our wee blether, she went off on one as she tried to explain something to me that had recently occurred.

'Ye know her alang the road wi' the three weans tae three different men that wis pregnet again? Well she had anither yin last week and it was wan o' yon miniature weans!'

'Miniature weans?' I asked.

'Aye, a miniature wean. Ye know whit ah mean . . . miniature.'

I looked at her with a puzzled expression and said, 'What, she gave birth to a midget?'

'Naw! No' a midget. A miniature wean . . . Ye know the kind! They're always wee scrawny things, God love them.'

'Aw-right!' I replied, starting to wind her up. 'You mean the wean was a dwarf?'

'Naw the wean's no' a dwarf!' she responded angrily. 'It's a bloody miniature wean – ye know fine well whit ah mean!'

I shook my head. 'No, I don't know what you mean, Mam!'

'Ye do so. A wean that didnae go the full distance!'

Now, I knew exactly what she was trying to say, but I kept winding her up. 'What full distance are you talking about? Where was it going to?'

'It wisnae going anywhere. It's already arrived here early, hence the reason it wis a miniature wean,' she replied angrily.

At that, I felt I had to put her out of her misery before she blew a fuse, so I said, 'I take it you mean the baby was born premature?'

Quick as a flash, she responded, 'That's it! It wis born premature . . . That's why it was a miniature!'

Porta Potty Time!
. . .

When a local ned attempted to siphon fuel from a motor home parked in Strathclyde Park, he got more than he bargained for.

The police arrived to find a very sick man, curled up next to a pool of spilled, mingin sewage.

A police spokesman said that the man admitted trying to steal fuel, but he'd plugged his siphon hose into the motor home's sewage tank by mistake.

The owner of the motor home declined to press charges, saying that it was the first time he'd heard of someone deliberately 'taking the piss'!

Oh, To Be Twelve Again

...

I was sitting on the edge of the bed one morning, observing my missus as she was looking at herself in the wardrobe mirror.

Since her birthday was coming up, I asked her what she would like as a surprise.

'I'd like to be twelve again!' she replied, while still looking at herself in the mirror.

A week later, on the morning of her birthday, I arose early, poured her a nice big bowl of Coco Pops, then fastened her into the car seat and drove her down to Strathclyde Park and paid her into the M&D theme park.

What a day! I put her on every ride in the park: the Death Slide, the Corkscrew, the Wall of Fear, the Screaming Monster Roller Coaster and the Big Dipper. You name it, I put her on it.

She even had pink candy floss and a heart-shaped lollipop.

Six hours later we staggered out of the theme park. Her head was reeling and her stomach felt upside down.

I then took her to Burger King where I ordered her a Kiddie Meal with extra fries followed by a large chocolate ice-cream decorated with Smarties.

After she'd finished, I whisked her off to the cinema to watch the latest 'Hanna Montana' movie, with popcorn, a huge Coca Cola drink, and a hot dog, her favourite.

What a fabulous day of fun and adventure!

Finally, I drove her back home, carried her into the house where she collapsed, totally exhausted, onto our bed.

I leaned over her with a big smile on my face and lovingly asked, 'Well, darling, how did it feel to be twelve again?'

As she slowly opened her eyes, her facial expression suddenly changed and she said, 'I meant my dress size, you retard!'

Harry's Polis News

•••

Police in Manchester have revealed that a woman has been arrested for shoplifting. Apparently she was found to have nicked a ten-inch salami sausage from a deli and concealed it down her knickers.

When asked to explain her actions, she replied it was because she was missing her Italian boyfriend, Romeo.

Aye right!

The Irish police are being handicapped in a search for a stolen van because they cannot issue a description of it.

Apparently it is a Special Branch vehicle and they don't want members of the public to know what it looks like!

So apparently, if you see it somewhere, you should keep its whereabouts to yourself.

Sounds like another old Irish joke . . . But it's true!

The Thriller!

...

Like every other workplace up and down the country, the big topic of conversation first thing every day before starting your shift is what a great book we have recently read, or film we have just watched.

I have to confess to being more of a viewer than a reader, as I have difficulty concentrating on the chapters in a book and find it easier to watch the action materialise on the screen.

During the shift muster, prior to being detailed our police duties, there was always someone who had read or watched something that should not be missed by the rest of the shift, and to reinforce his views on this, he would proceed to outline the storyline for us, prompting our interest in it, without giving away the entire plot, like a budding Barry Norman or Jonathan Ross!

It wasn't unusual to have several books with a page turned down marking the spot where the reader had left off, peppered around the office area, particularly in the rest rooms, where the on-duty shift would spend their forty-five-minute refreshment period totally engrossed in the latest chapter.

Not being an avid reader as explained, this was not my scene, as I preferred to hear someone describe the plot in detail, and preferably by someone who was good at telling a story and bringing it to life.

However, when charged with running an office for a few years, I did take great delight in reading the last chapter of many a book being read by a shift member, who would be totally engrossed in the characters and thrilling storyline, and while in conversation with them, I would nonchalantly 'spill the beans' regarding the plot outcome and reveal, in all innocence (not!) the ending of the book to them, twist in the tale and all!

Many of my colleagues would refer to me as being one without parents who were legally married, although others would consider it an innocent slip of the tongue.

Suffice to say none of them ever suspected I had only ever read the last part of their book – the part where all was revealed and the plot unravelled – while it was left lying about. They preferred to believe I'd actually read the storyline in its entirety.

I would very neatly and cleverly cut out the last or second-last page of the book which detailed the description in full of all the details pertaining to the plot and the clues to help solve it. Then, several weeks later, so that they wouldn't miss out, I would anonymously send the missing pages to them through the internal post!

On one particular occasion two of the cops on my shift were discussing a film that one of them had just seen and was giving a video copy to the other to view with his recommendation.

'You'll be glued to the screen, it's absolutely brilliant!'

'So it's worth watching then?' the other would ask.

'Most definitely. There's a twist at the end, pure brilliant!'

'So what's it called again?'

'*Presumed Innocent.*'

'Who's in it?'

'Harrison Ford, Greta Scacchi, Brian Dennehy and Bonnie Bedelia. It's a smashing cast.'

Just then, the cop lending the film was called away and the other cop walked over to where I was standing and was about to put it into his locker.

'Good film, Tam?' I asked.

'Apparently it is, Harry. It's a suspense thriller with Harrison Ford called *Presumed Innocent*.' He replied. 'Have you seen it?'

'Oh yes! Know the one, smashing film, great twist at the end,' I said. 'You'll never work it out.'

As he closed his locker and was about to leave, I couldn't resist it and shouted after him, 'By the way, Tam!'

As he turned back round to face me, I blurted out in my best mischievous voice, 'It was the wife!'

Children in Need

· · ·

A prominent QC was visited at his plush office by a volunteer from a children's charity organisation.

The charity representative began the meeting by saying, 'Our recent research shows that even though your annual income is in excess of £1.5 million, you don't give a penny to any charity. Wouldn't you like to give something back to your community by supporting our charitable work?'

The QC thought for a minute and said, 'Firstly, did your research also show you that my father is suffering from Alzheimer's and has accumulated huge private care nursing home bills that are far beyond his ability to pay?'

Embarrassed, the children's charity representative responded, 'Er . . . no, I didn't know that.'

'Secondly,' he said, 'are you aware that my brother, a disabled Gulf War veteran, is totally blind and confined to a wheelchair, and due to his disability, he is unable to support his wife and three children?'

The stunned representative began to stammer out an apology, but was cut off again.

'Thirdly!' continued the QC. 'Did your recent research also show you that my sister's husband was involved in a fatal road accident, leaving her destitute with a heavy mortgage and five children under the age of ten years, one of whom is disabled and another who suffers from learning disabilities and has to have daily private tutors who charge her an absolute fortune in fees?'

Now totally and utterly embarrassed, the representative said, 'I'm so sorry, I had no idea.'

At that the QC said, 'Well, now you know. And if I didn't give any of my money to them, what the hell makes you think I'm going to give it to you?'

Next!
. . .

When his .38 calibre hand gun failed to go off as he fired it at his intended victim during a hold-up, would-be gangster Jimmy 'The Shooter' Elliot did something that can only inspire wonder. He peered down the barrel of his gun and pulled the trigger again.

Guess what? This time it worked perfectly. KAH-BOOM!

Ohhh Donna!

...

The day finally arrived when policewomen were awarded equal pay. From then on they had to go out on uniform patrol in pairs.

On Sunday late shift in the city centre, there were only a few drinking places open, usually hotels.

Big Donna was a brand-new probationary constable straight out of Tulliallan Police College, and was being 'puppy walked' around the area by a senior policewoman when they received a call to assist with a large crowd leaving the Glassford Hotel.

En-route to the call, they came upon a disturbance involving two men fighting in the roadway.

They promptly took action and hand-cuffed the stand-up winner to the railings of a nearby public toilet.

Big Donna joined in by pulling up her tight skirt to her waist and jumping onto the chest of the loser, grabbing hold of his arms and pinning him to the ground.

On arrival of the police Land Rover, big Donna was screaming loudly, still on top of her accused, with her bare bum, black suspender belt and scanty panties fully exposed to the world, and with the accused male's head stuck between her buttocks.

Assistance was given, and both parties were separated, however big Donna wanted her accused further charged with sexual assault.

The accused was interviewed at the station where he stated, 'I genuinely thought she had hurt herself with her screaming in pain like that . . . I was only trying to soothe her pain.'

It was suggested to the accused that he plead guilty to the minor charge of a breach of the peace.

A week later, big Donna was being given 'private first-aid lessons' in her apartment by her off-duty shift sergeant, when he suffered a sudden heart attack.

An ambulance was called to attend and conveyed the sergeant to the hospital, completely naked – a new rule when learning first aid, I believe!

Big Donna, the loyal colleague that she was, remained by his side and accompanied him in the ambulance.

However, an anonymous caller contacted the off-duty shift sergeant's wife and informed her of his sudden illness.

The wife's attendance at the hospital, unfortunately for him, just happened to coincide with the arrival of big Donna, who was returning to the hospital with his neatly folded uniform.

'MEOUUWW!!'

Free Sex Competition

...

An independent petrol station owner in the south side of Glasgow was trying different ways to entice car owners into his garage to increase fuel sales.

As a result, he came up with the following idea and put up a large sign that read: 'Win Free Sex With Every Tank Full of Petrol!'

On seeing the sign, a local taxi driver pulled in, filled his tank up and asked for his free sex. The petrol station owner told him that he would pick a random raffle ticket from a bowl on his counter and if he picked one ending in a five, the taxi driver would get the offer of free sex. The proprietor picked out a raffle ticket, looked at it and said, 'It's an eight. Close, but not close enough. Sorry, but you haven't won free sex this time.'

A week later, the same taxi driver, along with his good friend and retired police officer, big Donnie Henderson, pulled in for another fill-up of petrol. After again filling up his tank, he asked for his free sex and the proprietor dipped his hand into the bowl filled with raffle tickets to pick out a number for him.

This time the taxi driver's number was announced as a seven by the garage proprietor, who quickly crumpled it up and threw it away before saying, 'Sorry, mate, you can't get into heaven with a number seven. It has to be a five to taste the honey from the hive. You were close, but I'm afraid there is no free sex this time. Do keep trying.'

As they left the garage and were driving away, the taxi driver turned to big Donnie and said, 'I think they bloody raffle tickets are rigged and he doesn't really give away free sex at all.' To which big Donnie immediately responded, 'Oh aye, he does. My wife won it twice last week and my daughter has won it once already this week!'

The Panda Car
• • •

A police officer was walking his beat one day when he noticed a small boy nearby in a little blue and white checked toy car, done up like a police panda car.

The boy was wearing a diced police helmet and his panda car was being pulled along by his two pet dogs.

The police officer walked over to him for a closer look.

'That sure is a nice police panda car you have there,' the policeman said with admiration.

'Thanks, Officer,' the boy replied.

The policeman looked a little closer and noticed that the boy had tied the front of the panda car to both his pet dogs' testicles.

'Excuse me, young man,' the policeman now said, 'I don't wish to tell you how to run your police panda car, but if you were to tie that rope around both your dogs' collars, I think you'll find that you could go much faster.'

The little boy looked up at the policeman standing there staring back at him and replied, 'With all due respect, Officer, you're probably right, but then I wouldn't have a siren.'

Wee Jock, Big Fight!

· · ·

Well I suppose it was bound to happen to wee Jock one day.

There he was, casually walking along the road, nonchalantly lifting his leg and watering every lamppost he came across, when suddenly, Bronson, a Staffordshire bull terrier, appeared from nowhere and jumped him, grabbing him around the neck and throwing him about like a Beanie Baby.

Taken totally by surprise, Jock had no chance, as Bronson waited for him to drop to the ground, before trapping him with his right paw and sinking his teeth into him several times in an attempt to rip his wee head clean off his body.

Fortunately, Jock was able to duck and weave to avoid Bronson getting a complete grip of him, and then there was good fortune for Jock as a police panda car stopped and a young blonde policewoman got out and rushed to his assistance, smacking Bronson over the head with her PR24 truncheon and chasing him away from the scene, thereby avoiding any more injuries being sustained by Jock.

Jock also tried to run off, before tripping up over his own legs and falling over in a heap – albeit, a small heap!

'Oh, you poor wee soul,' she said, as she bent over to lift him up. 'It's you, Jock, I recognise you now! Crikey, Jock, you're bleeding. Better get you to the nearest vet.'

At that, she placed Jock into the passenger seat and conveyed him to the local vet for treatment to his cuts.

'What happened to you then, Jock?' the vet asked.

'Ah got jumped!'

'Can you identify your attacker?' asked the vet.

'Naw! Nae chance. He jumped me from behind. Ah didnae see it coming, but I'll tell ye this much, he definitely had a real death wish. The big bastard made me look like a real Charlie!'

Unaware of all that had gone on before, I was in the house watching the TV when I heard a knock on the door.

I got up from my seat to open it, and was surprised to see the young blonde policewoman standing there holding a rather pathetic-looking Jock, feeling very sorry for himself.

'Is Jock your wee doggy?' she asked.

'Sort of,' I said. 'So what has he been up to now?'

'He hasn't been up to anything. Poor wee thing was attacked and beaten up. He was bitten that badly he had to be treated by the vet and have some stitches inserted into his wounds!'

'Is there a bill for all this?' I asked, concerned for the cost.

'No! Because I couldn't locate you earlier, I paid the bill for his treatment, so it's on me,' she replied.

At that she placed Jock down on the sofa and kissed the top of his head, while he whimpered like a puppy.

'The wee darling! If it's alright with you, Harry, I'll pop back in tomorrow to see how he is?'

'No problem, Officer, and thanks very much for bringing him home safely!' I said, closing the door behind her.

As I walked back into the lounge, Jock said, 'Dae me a favour, Harry, open up a can o' meat and chop it up for me?'

I walked over and was about to open the meat for him, when I thought, 'Wait a wee minute there, Jocky! Let's hear your version of what happened.'

'Nothing! I swear, it was a totally unprovoked attack!'

'Bollocks! Now tell me what really happened?' I said.

He looked up at me with his sad, sorry eyes. 'Okay! Ye know that Staffordshire bitch fae Busby that I was accused of giving one to? Well her brother obviously found out where I lived and was waiting to ambush me from behind and set about me. The vet said I've got more holes in my neck than a kitchen colander. All I can say is, he was very lucky I didn't see him coming!'

'So what are you going to do now?' I asked.

'Firstly, I'm gonnae get better, after which I'm going to get myself a personal trainer, like big Floyd up the next close!'

'You're not seriously telling me you're going into training to take on a Staffi terrier, are you?' I asked, fearing for his life.

'No way, Jose! I'm gonnae bribe Floyd with a big bone tae dae that.'

The Garden Plot!

· · ·

A widowed Glesca pensioner lived alone in the Carntyne area of the city. He wanted to plant his annual vegetable garden, but it was very difficult to do so, due to the ground being very hard to dig.

His only son, Frankie, who used to help him with this by preparing the ground for planting, was serving a custodial sentence in Barlinnie prison.

The old man decided to write him a letter describing his present predicament, hoping for a solution.

Dear Frankie,

I am feeling very sad, because for the first time in years, it looks like I won't be able to plant my vegetable garden. I'm just getting too old to be digging up a garden plot. I know if you were here, son, it would be no problem to you. I know how you enjoyed digging the garden for me, like in the old days.

What to do?

Love Dad

A few days later the old man received a letter back from his son.

Dear Dad,

For God's sake, whatever you do, don't even attempt to dig up the back garden. That's where all the bodies are buried!

Love Frankie

At six o'clock the following morning, the old man was awakened by forensic officers and uniformed police, arriving at his house, where they proceeded to dig up the entire garden area, without finding any bodies.

After several hours of searching, they made their apologies to the old man and left.

The very next day the old man received another letter from his son Frankie.

Dear Dad,

If everything has gone to plan, you should now be able to go ahead and start planting your vegetable garden.

That's the best I could do under the circumstances. Love you Dad,

Frankie.

Who said the prison authorities don't read your mail?!

OAP Femme Fatal

. . .

And here I thought it only happened in Glesca, but no matter where you go, and there are OAPs about, it'll happen.

Last week I was down in London, queuing up to purchase my Oyster Card in the post office and the little old lady in front of me let one drop. 'Bbblllerreuuuupppp!'

Nothing! No flicker of an eyebrow from her. Not even an apology and it was totally minging!

I immediately looked behind me apologetically, then thought to myself: Why? I didn't do it, but she made me feel guilty by her actions – or should I say, her lack of reactions.

I made the usual facial expressions, as you do, waving my hands in front of me before pointing the finger at her.

I tried to casually compose myself moments later, having dissipated the smell by my constant hand waving before returning to my position in the queue.

No sooner had I done this when, 'Bbbrrrrruuuuuuupppphh!' She farted again. The noise smothered out that of the annoying Royal Mail CD they play on the public side of the counter, while you wait your turn to be served.

This was followed by a horrible stench of bowfin', bowel flatulence, wafting its way through the customers in the queue.

'That was definitely not me!' I announced innocently, if not too convincingly. I pointed an accusing finger at the little ol' lady in front of me, in my attempt to divert any blame.

'It was her – honest!' I said, pathetically whispering.

The fact that the little old lady didn't bat an eyelid, or disturb a hair of her purple rinse, appeared to say it all, and no amount of pleading my innocence was going to convince my fellow queue members otherwise, even when, after being served, she looked at everyone in line with her pathetic wee face, apologised for taking so long, and then directed a big smile in my direction.

Glesca Euthanasia
. . .

Last night, my missus and I were sitting in the living room watching the telly and I just happened to turn to her and say, 'I never want to live in a vegetative state, where I'm dependent on some machine and fluids from a bottle. If you ever see that happening to me, just pull the plug.'

At that, she got up out of her seat, unplugged the TV, and poured my bottle of malt whisky down the sink.

She's such a bitch!

Exposed

• • •

It was a hot summer day and the newly appointed female Metropolitan Police Commissioner, who was very much a sun worshipper, decided to go up onto the roof of police headquarters for some much-needed sun bathing.

She lay down in a likely sun spot, but after a few minutes she saw the dark shadow of a nearby office building beginning to shade her legs.

She sat up and looked around for a better location, when she noticed to her right a large, clear flat area that couldn't be obstructed or overshadowed, so she moved over to it.

Settling down, she turned around slowly and noticed that there was no one around. Finding herself all alone, she proceeded to remove her blouse, then her suit skirt, laid face down with her head to one side, draped a towel across her bare bottom, and drifted off to sleep.

A short time later, she was aroused and slowly opened her eyes to see a pair of brightly polished shoes immediately in front of her.

She glanced up to see the headquarter's commissionaire, an officious-looking male officer in formal attire, standing at attention, carefully diverting his eyes to the side. 'Begging your pardon, ma'am,' he said stiffly. 'But I'm afraid you cannot sunbathe here'.

'And why not?' she asked. 'I'm up here by myself and I'm not bothering anyone.'

The commissionaire cleared his throat uncomfortably before replying, 'True, ma'am, but you're sunbathing face down on the glass roof of the headquarters canteen!'

Practical Jokers

...

The police force is just like any other job, where your fellow workers enjoy playing practical jokes, particularly on the latest recruits to join the shift.

Such was the case with Peter, who after completing his training was sent to work in Motherwell police station, where he walked the beat one night with his tutor cop Stuart.

About three a.m. they were walking past some shops and about to turn the corner when Stuart suddenly looked up and said, 'For fuck's sake, would you look at that daft bastard on the roof?'

Peter looked up towards the dark skies to see the silhouette of what looked like a naked man about to jump off the roof. This was followed by a male voice calling out, 'Don't try and stop me! Ah'm gonnae jump!'

Poor Peter, to witness an incident such as this on his first night on the beat, caused him to almost physically shit himself.

Worse was to follow, as moments later, the naked male jumped off the roof, hitting the road below, breaking into pieces.

Peter did not witness the landing, however, having closed his eyes tightly prior to the jumper making contact with the ground.

Almost fainting at the thought of it, he eventually opened his eyes to see Stuart and a few other police colleagues standing in front of him laughing hysterically at his reaction.

It appears that two other members from his shift had found an old mannequin at the rear of the local Burton clothes shop earlier on in the evening and, along with Stuart, they had arranged the special surprise for Peter the rookie!

They had climbed up the rear fire escape and balanced it on the edge of the roof, while holding it up with a rope until Stuart arrived with Peter, then let the rope go, for what was considered to be his initiation to the shift and a great practical joke!

Theology
. . .

My son is studying Theology and during a class at college, the students were instructed to write a short story in as few words as possible. The instructions were that the short story had to contain the following three things:

Religion
Sexuality
Mystery

And the winning story was: 'Good God, I'm pregnant. I wonder who did it!'

A Genuine Fake

· · ·

I recently went on holiday to Marmaris in Turkey and was amused by a sign outside a shop that advertised, 'Genuine Fake Watches!' Apparently by declaring this, it makes it legal to sell them.

For a fraction of the cost, you could purchase a fake Rolex, Tag Heuer, Breitling, you name it. Mind you, they probably wouldn't last for any length of time!

During my stay, I was speaking to an English couple who were also on holiday and we were talking about the number of fake items available to buy and he was saying that he'd asked one of the sellers if the Breitling watch he was offering for sale at twenty-five Euros actually worked. To which the trader replied, 'Don't be silly, sir. If it actually worked I would be asking for fifty Euros!'

A bit like the seller at a car boot sale who once offered to sell me the Beatles' famous 'White' album for the princely sum of £10.

While I mulled over his offer and was deciding whether to buy it or not for £10, he interrupted my contemplating by insisting, 'I'm dayin' ye a right favour here, big man. I've been offered £200 for it on Ebay!'

Well, you never know. Some people might have believed him!

Call me cynical, but I reluctantly declined his offer of doing me a 'right favour'!

Lucky White Heather
* * *

An off-duty police officer was working on his motorcycle on the patio at the rear of his house.

While running the engine, the motorcycle accidentally slipped into gear and, while still holding onto the handlebars, he was dragged along as it crashed through the double-glazed patio doors.

On hearing the crash, his wife ran into the room to find her husband cut and bleeding, lying across the damaged motorcycle and shattered patio door. She called for an ambulance to attend her husband.

While the paramedics were tending to him, the wife managed to push his motorcycle outside. (She was a big wummin!)

She also soaked up the spillage of petrol with some paper towels and disposed of them into the toilet.

After being treated by the paramedics, the off-duty policeman returned home, looked at the shattered patio door and the damage to his motorcycle.

He poured himself a large malt whisky, lit up a cigarette and disappeared into the bathroom to console himself while attending to his business.

Moments later, after he was finished, he stood up and flicked the cigarette butt between his legs.

Fortunately for him, his wife was nearby in the kitchen and heard the loud explosion, coupled with his screams of agony.

She rushed through to find him squirming about on the bathroom floor like a demented break dancer auditioning for 'Britain's Got Talent', with his trousers blown away and some serious burn marks on his bare buttocks, legs and groin.

Once again she contacted an ambulance and the same paramedic crew was dispatched to attend.

As the paramedics assisted her injured husband downstairs to the ambulance, they enquired from her as to how he had sustained the burns to himself.

After she told them, they both started laughing so hard, one of them slipped on the step, losing his grip of the stretcher, resulting in the husband falling down the remaining stairs, whereby he broke both his arms!

Now be honest, ye just couldn't make this up!

The Hypnotist

. . .

It was entertainment night at the local retired police officers' home.

Henry the hypnotist was booked for the night and declared, 'I'm here to put you into a trance and I intend to hypnotise each and every member of the audience.'

The excitement in the home amongst the residents was electric, as Henry withdrew from his waistcoat pocket a beautiful antique fob watch with rose gold chain.

'I want you all to focus your eyes on this antique watch. It's a very special watch and has been in my family for over six generations.'

At that, he began to swing the watch gently backwards and forwards while quietly chanting, 'Watch . . . the watch! Watch . . . the watch! Watch . . . the watch!'

The entire assembly of retired police officers were totally mesmerised by Henry as he swayed his beautiful antique watch backwards and forwards, with the light gleaming off its highly polished surface.

Hundreds of pairs of eyes followed the swaying watch until suddenly, disaster struck and it slipped from the hypnotist's hand and crashed onto the floor, shattering into a thousand pieces.

'SHIT!' blurted out the Hypnotist, loudly.

Which, if you think about it, under the present circumstances, was not exactly the best choice of word to use . . .

Apparently, it took three days to clean up the retirement home and they still can't get the smell out of the carpet!

A Glesca Cracker

• • •

This wee court story was sent to me by one of my ex-colleagues who swears to me that it's true!

The scene is the Glasgow High Court and the witness is a ned, being cross-examined by a new and rather politely spoken Advocate Depute (AD) on behalf of the Crown.

'You say you went out to your friends' house that night. Can you tell the court why you went there?' he asked.

'Ah went tae get a tap!' the ned replied.

'So is your friend a plumber?' asked the AD.

'Naw he's no' a plumber!'

'Are you a plumber then?' he asked.

'Naw! Ah'm no' a plumber either,' responded the ned, who was a bit bewildered by this line of questioning by the AD.

The AD then noticed the court police officer signalling to him and rubbing the fingers of one hand together in the universal gesture for money.

The penny dropped with the AD and he quickly changed his line of questioning accordingly.

'Ah, so you went to the house to borrow money?' he said.

'Naw!'

'So, you went to the house to lend money then?' he asked.

'Naw!' the ned again replied.

By this time the AD was totally exasperated and said, 'You told this court you went to your friends' house for a tap, so if it wasn't for a plumber or money, then what kind of tap was it?'

To which the ned replied in his total Glaswegian accent, 'A Sellick tap!'

(For those of you not fluent in the Glesca tongue, this loosely translated as, 'a Celtic football jersey'!)

Dope Story

• • •

One Glesca drug dealer is that cocky that when his clients phone up, his answering machine message says: 'Sorry I'm not available, but if you want to buy marijuana, please press the hash key . . .'

Earls Court Road

...

Having won first-class tickets for the Caledonian Sleeper, from Glasgow Central to London Euston, my wife and I set the date to go down for a week of West End shows.

Not exactly the best bit of planning I've ever done, with the Queen's tennis tournament on, Britney Spears at the O2 Arena, England national football team playing a World Cup qualifier against Andorra and the bloody Tube station workers on strike. It was absolute chaos!

However, lots of fun and games were to lie ahead.

Arriving off the sleeper, we had to drag the luggage outside the station and across the busy road to the bus stops where there were literally hundreds waiting to pounce on the first sight of a minute space on a big red bus. That's the way it was going to be.

Carrying around three heavy articles of luggage certainly slowed me down in the race to get on. Suddenly, I looked over to my left and noticed Sara Harkin, a friend from the BBC, who informed me she was down for a meeting. Fortunately for Sara, she was being met by the BBC transport vehicle. Unfortunately for us, there was no room for outsiders.

In the end we managed to squeeze ourselves onto the front of a bus and the driver didn't give a hoot when I plonked two of my pieces of luggage onto his front window ledge. He'd probably had enough hassle that day.

Thereafter, for the next hour or so, it was on bus, off bus as we weaved our way through the heavy London traffic to our hotel destination at Earls Court.

It was a hive of activity when we arrived and as a result, we had to wait for an hour to get into our room.

Sitting in the hotel foyer was a lesson in geography, as we racked our brains trying to work out the nationalities of the staff, which ranged from Asian, Romanian, Lithuanian, Australian, Russian, Canadian, Hungarian, Ukrainian and Austrian, with no English representatives to be seen.

And it didn't go unnoticed with me that their nationalities all ended in IAN! He must have been a more popular lover than Casanova around these parts!

Fire and Brimstone!

...

An ex-colleague was relating a story to me regarding his former partner in the police, who had been admitted to hospital for a simple operation.

Apparently while in the operating theatre having this routine procedure to remove a mole from his bottom, he broke wind during the operation and as a result set fire to his genitals when they were ignited by a spark from the laser instrument being used by the surgeon.

Worse was to follow, as the surgical spirits used to sterilise the area around his 'family jewels' caught fire.

No jokes please about being in the 'Burns' unit.

Due to his testicles now resembling two overcooked meatballs from *Gordon Ramsay's Kitchen Nightmares*, he is now suing the hospital.

He states that apart from his ongoing excruciating pain, he also suffers from a persistent itch to his Kojak area, due to his loss of pubic hair, and as a result is unable to have sex with his wife.

I am deliberately withholding his name, due to the number of disgusting offers his wife has received through *Facebook*, and on the phone, offering to assist her with sexual favours, since she appears to be missing out, due to the old 'bald eagle' having barbecued his meat and two veg to a frazzle!

Fishing Weekend

• • •

Alex and Roy both worked as partners on the police divisional crime car for several years.

One weekend while off duty together they decided to go fishing. They loaded up Alex's motorbike and headed off up north.

After riding for a few hours, they got caught in a torrential downpour. Soaked to the skin, they pulled into a nearby farm and asked the lady who answered the door to them if they could spend the night there, while they dried off.

The lady was very hospitable toward them and said, 'I hate the idea of having you stay outside during this terrible weather, but I live here all by myself, due to the fact that my husband has only recently passed away,' she explained. 'But I'm afraid my neighbours would talk if I let you stay in the house with me a lonely widow and living all alone.'

'No worries, ma'am,' Alex said. 'We'll be only too happy to sleep in the barn and dry off, and if the weather breaks early, we'll be on our way.'

The lady agreed, and the two cops found their way to the barn and settled down for the night.

Bright and early the following morning, the weather had eased off, and Alex and Roy left to continue on their journey.

They enjoyed the next few days of fishing. However, about ten months later, Alex was to receive an unexpected letter from a reputable solicitors' office in Inverness.

It took him a few minutes to figure it out, but he finally determined that it was from the firm of solicitors representing the attractive elderly widow he had met on the fishing weekend.

Later the same day, he dropped in at the police station on his colleague and asked, 'Roy, do you remember that good-looking lady from the farm we stayed at on our fishing trip up north about ten months ago?'

'Yes, I do,' replied Roy, somewhat hesitantly.

'Tell me this – did you . . . er . . . happen to get up during the night, and go up to the house and pay her a visit while she was sleeping, all alone in that big house?'

'Eh, well . . . erm . . . yes I did as a matter of fact!' Roy said, slightly embarrassed about being found out.

'I have to admit that I did, but I was going to tell you about it, honest.'

'Is that right?' Alex asked. 'And did you just happen to give her my name and address instead of your own when you left her that morning?'

Roy's face turned beetroot red as he blushed uncontrollably and said, 'Yeah, I'm sorry, buddy, I'm afraid I did. But I can explain, it was . . . 'Then he paused before continuing. 'Wait a minute, why are you asking all this?'

To which Alex responded, ''Cause apparently she died last month and left everything to me in her will!'

Number-Four Idiot

• • •

A guy walked into a little corner store armed with a shotgun and ordered the female assistant to put all of the money from the cash drawer into a bag.

The assistant did as she was told, when the robber saw a bottle of whisky that he liked on the shelf behind the counter and ordered her to put it into his bag as well. But the assistant refused, saying, 'I'm sorry, but I don't believe you're over twenty-one years of age.'

The robber argued that he was, but the female assistant still refused to hand it over, stating she didn't believe him.

At this point, the robber put his shotgun down on the counter, took his driver's licence out of his wallet and handed it over to the cashier to check it out as proof of his age.

The cashier looked it over and agreed that he was in fact over twenty-one years, and put the bottle of whisky into the bag. After which, the robber ran off from the store with his loot.

The cashier promptly contacted the local police and supplied them with the full name and address of the robber, which she had noted from his driving licence.

Surprise! Surprise!

On his arrival home, he walked in the front door to find two armed police officers sitting in the front room of his parents' house waiting to arrest him for the robbery.

He still hasn't worked out how they knew where to come for him!

This is one guy who definitely needs to wear a big sign.

Choking

...

A father walked into a plush restaurant with his young son and handed him three pennies to play with to keep him occupied.

Suddenly, the boy started choking and going blue in the face.

The father immediately realised that his boy had swallowed the pennies and started slapping him on the back.

The boy coughed up two of the pennies, but continued choking. Looking at his son, the father panicked and called for help.

At that, a well-dressed, attractive and serious-looking woman in a grey business suit, sitting at the coffee bar reading a newspaper and sipping a cup of coffee, looked up from her seat at the sound of commotion, put her coffee cup down, neatly folded her newspaper then got up from her seat and made her way across the floor of the restaurant.

Reaching the distressed boy, the woman carefully unzipped his trousers, grabbed hold of his testicles and started to squeeze and twist them, gently at first and then ever so firmly.

Moments later the boy began convulsing violently and coughed up the last penny, which the woman deftly caught in her free hand.

Releasing her grip of the boy's testicles, the woman then handed the penny over to his father and casually walked slowly back to her seat at the coffee bar without saying a word.

As soon as he was sure that his son had suffered no ill effects, the father walked over to the woman and thanked her, saying, 'I've never seen anybody do anything like that before, it was quite amazing to watch. Are you a doctor or a nurse?'

'No!' the woman replied. 'I'm a divorce lawyer!'

Half Past Four

• • •

A retired inspector was talking to his next-door neighbour and telling him, 'I just got fitted with a new hearing aid today. Apparently it's state of the art technology and cost the NHS two thousand pounds. It's absolutely amazing. Even the slightest of noises is crystal clear!'

'Really?' said his neighbour. 'So, what company makes them then?'

'Who, Mary? She's on the phone talking to my daughter.'

Jury Duty Excuse

· · ·

This is a true Affidavit that was sent back to the court's jury service on 26 January 2009.

They send out an Affidavit to a named person who has been selected for jury duty and the named person then has to fill out the form and return it with an explanation why they should be excused from such duty.

The Affidavit is laid out thus: *Request to be excused from Jury Service for case at issue.*

I, Harry the Polis, being first duly sworn upon oath, depose and say that jury service would entail undue hardship on me and that I request to be excused from jury service for the following reasons . . .

You then submit your reason in writing.

This is one that was received by the jury service staff: *'Apparently you morons didn't understand me the first time.*

I CANNOT take time off from my work and I'm not putting my family's well-being at stake to participate in this load of crap.

I don't believe in our 'Legal Justice' system and I don't want to have a goddamn thing to do with it.

Jury duty is a complete waste of time.

I would rather count the wrinkles on my dog's bollocks than sit on a jury.

Get it through your thick skulls and leave me the hell alone!'

I think this potential juror is very articulate in his use of the English vocabulary and explains himself very well under the circumstances – therefore he should definitely be excused jury duty!

Breaking News

• • •

Strathclyde Police cordoned off Greenock town centre this morning when a suspicious object was observed in a car.

It later turned out to be a valid tax disc.

Dumb! Dumb!

...

I once received a call to attend the Royal Infirmary Accident and Emergency Department regarding a young blonde woman being admitted late one night with the tip of her index finger missing after a gunshot accident.

The woman did not wish to explain how the accident happened, so it was left to me to question her about it.

'How did this happen?' I began by asking her.

She sat there for a moment contemplating, reluctant to speak with me, then suddenly she opened her mouth and I couldn't stop her.

'Well, believe it or not, I was trying to commit suicide,' she replied.

'What?' I responded, shocked by her explanation. 'You tried to commit suicide, so you shot your finger off?'

She shook her head and said, 'No, no, no, you silly man. 'Firstly, I pointed the gun at my chest, and then I thought, "I've just spent £5,000 getting these breast implants fitted. I'm certainly not going to shoot myself there."'

'So, what next?' I asked her.

'Well then I put the gun into my mouth, and I thought, "wait a minute there, Mandy, you've just paid £4,000 to get these teeth straightened and whitened. You're not shooting yourself in the mouth!" I mean to say . . . what a waste of money that would have been. Don't you agree?'

'Yes! So, what did you do then?' I asked, eager for her to continue.

'Well that's when I decided to put the gun up to my ear, and just as I was about to pull the trigger, I thought, "this is bound to make a very loud bang. So, in order not to deafen myself, I put my other finger up to my ear before I pulled the trigger . . . '

Did I mention that this girl was blonde?

What a Load . . .

. . .

A young woman driver was pulled over by the police for speeding in a built-up area.

As the traffic cop walked up to her car window, he flipped open his ticket book, and before he uttered a word, the female driver said, 'I bet you're going to ask me to buy a ticket to the Strathclyde Police Ball.'

Without the slightest hesitation, he promptly blurted out, 'Strathclyde Police don't have any balls!'

At that, there was a moment's silence, when she smiled at him and he considered his impromptu response to her question. He then closed over his ticket book and without saying another word, returned to his police car and promptly drove off.

As for the female driver, she couldn't drive her car for laughing!

Car Trouble

. . .

This was apparently an article in the *Daily News*, supplied by an anonymous police officer in the West Midlands, about an off-duty colleague and his wife who drove their car to the local Asda Superstore to buy their weekly groceries.

However, just as they were about to park within the car park, their car broke down.

The off-duty cop told his wife to carry on with the shopping while he fixed the problem with the car.

The wife went off to carry out his instructions, returning a short time later to see a small group of people near the car.

Taking a closer look herself, she saw a pair of hairy legs protruding from under the front of the car.

Unfortunately, although wearing a pair of fashionable shorts, he was unaware that his lack of underwear resulted in his 'family jewels' being publicly exposed for all to see.

Unable to stand the embarrassment of her husband's genitals fully exposed in a public car park, she dutifully stepped forward, knelt down and quickly put her hand up his shorts, in order to tuck everything back into place and out of sight from the assembled crowd.

On regaining her feet, she glanced across the car bonnet to find herself face to face with her policeman husband, who was standing, watching with everyone else, all that was taking place.

Suffice to say, the RAC mechanic received such a fright when she was performing her good deed to preserve his modesty that he banged his head on the car chassis frame and had to have three stitches inserted to his forehead.

The Loving Husband

· · ·

My former police colleague Robert Ball, who is a fanatical Rangers supporter, had two of the best tickets for the Homecoming Scottish Cup Final.

As he took his seat at Hampden Park, a supporter came along and asked if anyone was sitting in the vacant seat next to him with a better view.

'No!' he replied. 'This seat is most definitely empty.'

'This is wonderful!' the other supporter enthused. 'Who in their right mind would have bought a ticket for the Homecoming Scottish Cup Final, the biggest sporting event of the year in Scottish football, and not turn up to take their seat?' Robert replied, 'Well, actually, the seat you are sitting in belongs to me. My wife was supposed to accompany me to the match, but unfortunately, she passed away recently.

'This is the first Cup Final we haven't been to together since we got married.'

'Oh . . . I'm so sorry to hear that. That's just terrible.'

There was a pause of a moment's silence, before the other supporter enquired, 'I guess you couldn't find someone else, like a friend or relative, or even a neighbour to accompany you to the game and take her seat?'

Robert shook his head and replied, 'Unfortunately not. They're all attending her funeral!'

Dr Feelgood

· · ·

My son, who wants to be a doctor, was working with a GP in Govan, getting some work experience, when the GP said, 'Listen, Kayed, I've been watching how well you've been getting on with the patients and I thought, since you're doing so well, rather than close up the clinic, you could maybe take care of it yourself and see to all my patients, while I went fishing this afternoon.'

'Definitely, sir!' replied Kayed.

That settled, the GP went off to do some fishing.

The following day, on his return the GP asked, 'So, Kayed, tell me, how was your day in charge?'

Kayed informed him that he had taken care of three patients. 'The first one had a headache, so I prescribed him Panadol.'

'Well done, mate, and the second one?' asked the GP. 'The second one had stomach burning, so I prescribed him Losec to take, sir,' said Kayed.

'Excellent diagnosis! You're very good, and what about the third one?' he asked.

'Well, sir, I was sitting here at the desk when suddenly the door opened and a woman entered. Before I could stop her, she undressed herself, taking off everything, including her bra and her pants. She then lay down naked on the table and shouted, 'Help me, Doctor! I haven't seen a man in over two years!'

The GP looked over at him in amazement, settled down in his chair and said, 'So, come on then. Tell me, what did you do?' he asked, desperate to hear the sordid details.

To which Kayed replied in all sincerity, 'Simple! I washed both her eyes out with Optrex drops.'

Sorry about the ending folks, but my boy isn't like that and doesn't think like you lot out there!

Or me, for that matter!

The Car Boot

· · ·

I was enjoying my favourite pastime the other day, walking around a car boot sale, and I came across a female stall holder who was advertising the price of her goods for sale.

'Everything's a pound! Only a pound! Grab a bargain! Help yersel' tae anything ye see for only a pound!'

On hearing this offer, I bent down and picked up a book.

Quick as a flash, on seeing me with the book in my hand, she shouted over, 'That book's two pound, darling!'

What's in a Name?

• • •

This was sent to me in an email by an ex-colleague, and I enjoyed it that much, I had to include it for you.

After the untimely death of Quasimodo, the Bishop of Notre Dame Cathedral sent word through the streets of Paris that a new bell-ringer was required to take over the duties.

The Bishop decided that he would conduct the interviews personally and went up into the belfry to begin the screening process.

After observing several applicants as they demonstrated their bell-ringing skills, he had decided to call it a day when an armless man approached him and announced that he was there to apply for the bell-ringer's job.

The Bishop was incredulous. 'You have no arms!'

'Not a problem,' said the man. 'Please, observe!' And he began striking the bells with his face, producing a beautiful melodic sound on the carillon.

The Bishop listened in disbelief, convinced he had finally found a replacement for Quasimodo. But suddenly, as he lunged forward to strike a bell, the armless man tripped and plunged headlong out of the belfry window onto the grey cobbled streets below, to his death.

The stunned Bishop rushed to his side and as he reached his broken body, a crowd had gathered around the fallen figure, drawn by the beautiful music they had heard only moments earlier.

As the Bishop stood over him, one of crowd asked, 'Bishop, who was this man?'

The Bishop sadly replied, 'I don't know his name . . . But his face rings a bell!'

WAIT! WAIT! There's more . . . Read on . . .

The very next day, despite all the sadness that weighed heavily on his heart due to the unfortunate death of the armless campanologist (that's bell ringer to you), the Bishop of the cathedral continued with his task of interviewing candidates for the position of bell-ringer of Notre Dame.

The first man to approach him said, 'Your Excellency, I would like to introduce myself, I am the brother of the recently deceased, armless wretch that fell to his death from this very belfry only yesterday.

'I pray that you will honour his life and that of his family, by allowing me to replace him in this duty.'

The Bishop immediately agreed to give the man an audition.

The armless man's brother took up his position and stooped to pick up the mallet in order to strike the first bell, when suddenly he made a groaning noise, clutched at his chest, twirled around, before dropping down dead on the spot.

Two monks, on hearing the bishop's cries for help at this second tragedy in as many days, rushed up the stairs to assist him.

'What has happened, Your Excellency? Who is this man lying before you?' the first monk asked breathlessly.

'I don't know his name,' sighed the distraught Bishop. 'All I know is . . .

(Wait for it . . .)

(It's well worth it!)

' . . . He's the dead ringer for his brother!'

Bogus Grannies

. . .

A young police probationer was out shopping in a super-market when he noticed an old woman following him around the store. If he stopped, she would stop and stare at him.

Finally, she overtook him at the lane for the checkout, and turned to him and said, 'I do hope I didn't make you feel embarrassed or uneasy, but it's just that you look so much like my late son in your uniform – he was also a police officer.'

The young police officer replied, 'Not at all, it's perfectly fine.'

She then said, 'I know it sounds awfully silly, but do you think you could call out, "Goodbye, Mum" as I leave the store? It would be such a nice gesture and make me feel so very happy.'

'Why certainly, ma'am, no problem,' responded the obliging young officer.

At that, she turned and walked over to the checkout.

She smiled and chatted with the supermarket cashier as he looked on, and as she was on her way out of the store, the young police officer called out after her, loud and clear across the busy checkouts, 'Goodbye, Mum.'

The old woman gave a wave of her hand and smiled back at him.

Moments later and pleased that he had brought a little piece of sunshine into someone's day, he went over to the checkout to pay for his shopping.

'That comes to a total of £63.85,' said the store assistant. 'What!' asked a shocked and surprised young officer. 'How come it's so much? I've only bought five items.'

The store assistant replied, 'Yes, but your mother said you'd be paying for her messages as well!'

The Milky Way

· · ·

Ivan Jackson was a milkman prior to joining the police and one nightshift while we were working together he told me this story.

Apparently a blonde woman heard that if she soaked in a bath of milk, it would make her beautiful. So before going to bed, she left a note for Ivan the milkman to leave her twenty-five gallons of milk.

The following morning, when Ivan read the note, he thought to himself, 'There must be a mistake here.'

He worked out that she probably meant 2.5 gallons. So he knocked on her front door to clarify the point.

The blonde woman answered the door and Ivan said, 'I found your note asking me to leave twenty-five gallons of milk. I take it you meant two and a half gallons?'

The blonde woman said, 'No! I want twenty-five gallons. I'm going to fill up my bath and soak in the milk, so that I can look young and beautiful again.'

Ivan looked at her and asked, 'Do you want it pasteurised?'

To which the blonde woman replied, 'No, just up to my tits. I can splash it on my face if I need to.'

London Underground

. . .

I was recently down in London for a few days and, like most people, I travelled around using the underground.

While doing so, I was highly entertained by some of their control room announcers, who I found very witty and amusing.

On leaving Euston Square station, I mentioned this to a ticket collector, who immediately went into his inside pocket and handed me a list with some of the best comments recorded:

'Ladies and Gentlemen, I do apologise for the delay to your service. I know you're all dying to get home, unless, of course, you happen to be married to my ex-wife, in which case you'll want to cross over onto the westbound line and go in the opposite direction.'

'Please allow the doors to close. Try not to confuse this with "Please hold the doors open." The two are distinctly different instructions.'

'Please note that the beeping noise coming from the doors means that the doors are about to close. It does not mean throw yourself or your bags into the doors.'

'We can't move off because some idiot has their hand stuck in the door.'

'To the gentleman wearing the long grey coat trying to get on the second carriage – what part of "stand well clear of the doors" don't you understand?'

No Complaint

• • •

I answered a call on the nightshift to attend a complaint of assault in the deprived high flat area of Sighthill, Glasgow.

The victim was a female who informed me that her boyfriend had just been released from prison after serving a three-month custodial sentence for assaulting her and decided to have a 'getting out' party at the local pub.

After several hours of celebrating, with lots of alcohol being consumed, he went home with her to make up for lost time, with sex on his mind.

Unfortunately for him, it was the last thing on her mind and as a result, a full-scale argument ensued, followed by the female being assaulted by her horny, drunken, ex-jail-bird of a boyfriend, who then buggered off sharpish, prior to my arrival.

The next-door neighbour, who just happened to be her gay brother, was a witness to the incident and insisted on giving a statement of the events. However, after noting his statement, he continued to express his views regarding what the police should be doing about the physical assault on his sister.

Due to his continual interference and arrogant behaviour, which was bordering on a breach of the police, he was requested to return to his own flat, but refused. Therefore, I had no alternative but to apprehend him for refusing to comply with my request to leave and led him outside, where I hand-cuffed him to a large drainage pipe in the corridor outside.

I then returned to speak with the complainer and finish off noting her statement.

Surprise! Surprise! When I returned to the hand-cuffed brother outside, he was standing there bollock-naked, with his trousers down at his ankles. He then alleged that he had been sexually abused by two males while he waited patiently outside, still hand-cuffed to the pipe and unable to resist.

As he was only outside his sister's door, and my colleague and I were within earshot, I asked why he hadn't called out for us to come and help him?

He replied, 'Tae tell ye the truth, big man, I didnae know if you two would have helped me, or just took yer place in the queue. By the way, I hope you don't think I'm a slut, dae ye?'

After a cooling-down period, the accused/victim gay brother remarked, off the record: 'If her man had came back wi' me when I offered, I could have relieved his tension and this would never have happened tae any of us!'

T.M.I. there!

As a result, a warning was given as to his future conduct and he was quite happy to forget about his alleged assault, putting it down to experience.

As a result it was related to the police controller regarding the incident: 'No police action required; complainer(s) satisfied with the result!'

Organic Health Drinks

• • •

Once again summer is looming and with it comes the good weather, exotic holidays and that dreaded fitness regime to try and lose weight, look healthy and feel good.

My missus has decided that we are going organic – and I mean everything, from sugar to cream crackers, from apples to lettuce and from milk to bread, has got to be organic!

Not only that, she has now bought us a juicer and makes these recipes for us to drink, all of which are meant to be good for you . . . Allegedly!

Yesterday morning I was awakened by her dulcet tones crying out to me that breakfast was ready.

I stumbled through to the kitchen in expectation that my nose buds were not working properly and I was about to witness an odourless plate, consisting of a full Scottish breakfast with square sausage, Ayrshire bacon, two fried eggs, fried tomatoes, mushrooms, black pudding and a tattie scone dripping wi' grease.

Shock, horror! There sitting waiting for me was a tall glass of green goocy stuff that wouldn't have looked out of place at the bottom of a stagnant fish pond full of algae!

'What is that?' I asked her as I slowly rotated the glass, trying to work out the ingredients, while also checking out the black bits and if there was still life there.

'It's your new organic health drink. Very good for you and full of vitamins, minerals and especially B17!' she replied.

'There's tadpoles in there,' I said.

'Where?' she said, checking the glass. 'No there is not, that's apple and pear seeds. Apparently they're very good for you too. Now go on, drink it down,' she ordered me.

I looked around the kitchen. 'Where's yours?' I asked.

'Gone! I drank it earlier,' she replied. 'Mmm, yummy, yummy, very nice!' she said, rubbing her tummy. 'Now hurry up and drink it, you big girl's blouse.'

That was hurtful. So I grabbed hold of the glass, raised it to my mouth and began gulping it down . . . Woahhhh! My throat began to close over.

'What the hell is in this? Is it dead yet? What's that horrible taste? Tell me. For the sake of the post-mortem certificate detailing the cause of death . . . Tell me what I just drank!'

'Oh, behave yourself. You're acting like big a drama queen!' she responded, while I was retching and boaking into the sink.

'You'd think I was trying to poison you, instead of getting you into some healthy eating!'

'Just tell me what was in it,' I asked – nae, pleaded!

She paused for a moment before rapidly listing the following ingredients: 'Kale, spinach, celery, ginger, onion, cabbage, seaweed, an apple, a pear and a clove of garlic! All very good for you,' she added.

'Good for me! My throat's on fire. I would have rather drank the entire contents of a colostomy bag! This is bloody murder!'

'Oh, don't exaggerate. I drank one as well,' she said.

'You never drank a glass of that. Admit it?' I said.

'Well, maybe not a full glass.'

'How much?' I asked. 'Tell me. How much?'

She put on that innocent-girlie look that women have mastered since childbirth and whispered very quietly her response. 'A half!'

'Speak up, I can't hear you. Now how much did you drink?'

'A mouthful!' she muttered.

'A mouthful? How much?' I pressed her for a real answer.

'Okay! I took a sip and spat it down the sink . . . Happy now?'

'A sip?' I said loudly.

'A sip!' she repeated. 'And this is the thanks I get for trying to get you to eat healthy. Well thanks very much, Harry.'

At that she stormed out of the kitchen, in true drama-queen style.

However, I have to admit, after the burning throat and stomach cooled off and settled, I visited the toilet several times over the next few days and as a result, reduced my overall weight by about five pounds. Scottish Slimmers would be proud of me.

The drawback was severe flatulence, and over the next two weeks, my backside made more noises than the *Last Night at the Proms* – although I hasten to add, not all of the notes were in the right place, and not all could be heard at the same time!

As a footnote to this, I visited my local pub later the same week for a quiet beer. I should be so lucky!

As I stood at the bar sipping on my Belhaven Best, I felt

an eruption bubbling away in my stomach, culminating in an explosion of wind bursting to escape past the cheeks of my bottom. As the music was really loud I relaxed my muscles, opening my bomb doors and nonchalantly letting rip, blasting off like a four-bob rocket on the 5th of November, with each drum and symbol beat of the music muffling the explosive sound like a professional percussionist, in perfect harmony and timing with the melody.

Eventually, I finished squeezing out my last blast of wind, which coincided with the music reaching its crescendo.

Finale over, I drank down the last of my beer, placed my glass down on the counter and turned around to see everybody in the bar staring at me with utter disgust etched across their faces.

It was at that precise moment I thought, SHIT! Especially when I suddenly realised I had been listening to my iPod!

Finally, let me try and clear up any misconceptions you might have had about health foods and healthy diets. And please remember, I'm no expert.

Life should NOT be a short journey to the grave with the intention of arriving there safely, in an attractive and well-preserved body, but the complete opposite. You should be slipping and sliding in sideways with a large malt whisky in one hand, a bar of Galaxy chocolate in the other, a thick 'Jimmy Saville' Havana cigar sticking out from the side of your gub, (men only) and a body that is totally and thoroughly blootered, completely worn out and screaming at the top of your voice, 'YEE-HAH! WHAT A RIDE!'

Always Say Thank You

. . .

If you have ever purchased something that has exceeded your expectations, then it is always nice to let the company who manufactures the product know. Such was the case with this particular lady . . .

I feel compelled to write to you and say what an excellent product you have in the market place!

I've used it all of my married life, because my mother always referred to it as being the best!

Now that I am in my mid-fifties, I find it better than ever. In fact, only about a month ago, I accidentally spilled some Merlot wine on my new white blouse.

My inconsiderate and uncaring husband immediately began to verbally abuse me about how clumsy I was, and generally started becoming a pain in the neck.

One thing led to another and somehow most of what happened is a blank, however I ended up with his blood all over my new white blouse!

I reached for my bottle of Vanish with bleach alternative, and to my surprise and complete satisfaction, all the stains came out! In fact, the blood stains came out so well, the detectives told me that the DNA tests on my blouse were totally negative and shortly after that, my attorney called to say I was no longer considered a suspect in the disappearance of my husband.

What a relief that was!

Going through the menopause is bad enough without being a murder suspect!

I thank you, once again, for having a first-class product. Well, as they say in Russia, Mos-cow, as I have to write a letter to B&Q thanking them for their heavy-duty refuse bags.

Bye for now.

A Very Merry Widow!

Don't Say It!
• • •

For those of you who like to watch what you eat, here's a word of warning on nutrition and health. It's a relief to know the truth after all those conflicting nutritional studies.

Apparently the Japanese eat very little fat and suffer fewer heart attacks than the British.

The Mexicans eat a lot of fat and suffer fewer heart attacks than the British.

The Chinese drink very little red wine and suffer fewer heart attacks than the British.

The Italians drink a lot of red wine and suffer fewer heart attacks than the British.

Even the blooming Germans drink a lot of beer and eat lots of sausages and plenty fat, and suffer fewer heart attacks than the British.

Having studied the statistics of this lot, I've decided to eat and drink whatever I like. It's speaking English that apparently kills you.

They're Coming . . .
. . .

A wee elderly Glesca man, living in the old tenements of the Gorbals, went to the local chapel for confession one day.

'Bless me, Father, 'cause ah huv sinned, big time.'

When the priest slid open the panel in the confessional, the wee man continued.

'It's like this, Father . . . During World War Two, a beautiful wee Polish lassie fae alang the road chapped on my door. She was screaming hysterically and asked me tae hide her fae the Nazis, 'cause she'd heard they had invaded Scotland. Ah knew her auld mammy had recently popped her clogs and she wis staying in the hoose hersel', so instinctively ah took her in and hid her up in ma loft!'

The priest replied: 'That was a wonderful, kind, humane thing you did, and you have no need to confess. You did what you thought was right under the circumstances.'

'Aye, but there's more tae tell ye, Father. Ye see, she started to repay me with sexual favours, know whit ah mean? This happened several times a week, and sometimes twice on a Saturday, if the "Sellick" were playing away from home.'

The priest said, 'That was a long time ago, and by doing what you did and by taking her in and making her feel safe, if it had been true, her actions of coming to your door could have placed the two of you in great danger. But with two people under those circumstances, one can easily succumb to the weakness of the flesh. However, if you are truly sorry for your actions, you are indeed forgiven!'

'Aw thanks, Father. That's a right load aff my mind. Ah dae huv one more question for ye though.'

'And what is that, my son?' asked the priest.

'Dae ye think it's aboot time ah telt her the war is over?'

The Alarm Clock

· · ·

One night I accompanied my police partner Alec Craig to his house in the early hours of the morning, during a nightshift.

He invited me in, and as I followed him into the lounge area, I couldn't help but notice that he had a massive big brass gong about five feet in diameter, sitting in the middle of his room.

'What's that?' I asked.

'That?' he said, pointing to the large gong. 'That's my alarm clock!'

'Your alarm clock? How does it work?' I asked.

'Easy. You just hit it. Watch, out the way and I'll show you,' he said as he picked up a large wooden club hanging from the side of it and raising it above his head. He brought it crashing down against the gong, making a deafening 'bong-g-g!' noise that vibrated off the walls of the house for several seconds.

Moments later, his next-door neighbour could be heard shouting out, 'Ho! Keep the noise down. It's two o'clock in the bloody morning!'

He then checked his wrist watch, held his arm out in front of me to see, looked me straight in the face, winked his eye and said, 'Spot on. Works every time!'

The Golf Outing

• • •

My good friend and resident nutter, big Donnie Henderson, along with three of his police colleagues, arranged to meet up for a game of golf.

They walked onto the course and after playing only three holes, they were held up while waiting for a particularly slow group of golfers in front of them.

One of the cops in Donnie's party said, 'What's with these guys? We've been waiting for about fifteen minutes now!'

Another remarked, 'I've never seen such crap golfers!'

The third cop shouted out, 'Ho! Gonnae move it, we've got our work to go to!'

Then the first cop said, 'Hold on, here comes Derek the greens keeper. Let's have a word with him about them.'

'Ho Derek!' he said. 'What's the score with that mob ahead of us? They're a bit slow, are they not?'

Derek the greens keeper looked over at the group and replied, 'Oh, that group? They're all blind fire fighters. They lost their sight while saving our clubhouse from a fire last year, so the club allows them to play the course for free anytime.'

The police officers all fell silent for a moment, before one of them said, 'God forgive me for complaining about them!'

A second one said, 'I'm going to contact my brother in law, he's an ophthalmologist, and see if there's anything he can suggest that could help them.'

The third one replied, 'I think I'll do a charity run for

them and try and raise some money in honour of their bravery.'

Donnie thought for a few moments then looked at his three colleagues standing there and said, 'So they're blind? Well how the hell can they no' play at night?'

Big Broon!

* * *

Stationed at Viewpark, Uddingston, was a big six-foot-six gentleman polis called Jimmy Brown – or 'Big Broon' as he was affectionately referred to by his colleagues.

Apparently during the Peter Manuel murder enquiry, a certain Willie Muncie was in charge of the Lanarkshire investigations and turned up unexpectedly at the station to brief his men. After the briefing, he decided to perform an impromptu inspection of them and their equipment.

The officers lined up and were instructed to produce their appointments for inspection.

As he walked along the line with each officer holding out their 'appointments' of whistle, hand-cuffs and baton, he stopped at Big Broon and asked, 'Where's yer cuffs, Broon?'

Nervously, Big Broon replied with the first thing he could think of, which just happened to be totally unrelated. 'Erm, I've a wee hole in my pocket, sir!'

Mr Muncie looked at him with a puzzled expression on his face before replying, 'Ye've a wee hole in your arse as well, Broon, but what has that got to do with you not having yer cuffs?'

The Police Marksman

· · ·

Police marksman and former colleague of mine John Knox was instructed to attend a call from a circus owner, regarding one of his Bengal tigers that had escaped from its cage in the Kelvin Hall Arena and was now running wild.

John arrived at the scene with his firearm, with specific orders to shoot the animal, should it become a danger to any members of the public.

As the circus owner, Bobby Roberts, and his staff searched the area for the tiger's whereabouts, it wasn't long before it was sighted at the rear of the Transport Museum nearby, where they managed to isolate it and prevent it from going any further.

Try as they might, the circus owner and his staff were having difficulty capturing the tiger, which was now baring its large ferocious teeth and preparing to wreak havoc.

With all efforts to capture the tiger proving unsuccessful, and the possible danger it posed to the public at large, the harsh decision was taken for the police marksman to take over and deal with the situation.

Prior to John taking up his best position to have a clear shot at the tiger, Bobby Roberts passed on some last-minute advice to him.

'I'm not going to lead you up the garden path here. We have a serious situation, because this is one ferocious tiger. He attacked my last animal tamer and savaged him. His injuries were so bad, he required 470 stitches, skin grafts to his face and body, as well as having his right arm ripped from the socket. So, when you take aim to shoot it, you had better be good, or you're history!'

A few moments later, John was lining up his sights when a young, blonde woman wearing a long black coat walked straight past him carrying a small stool and a whip.

She walked in front of his gun sights and towards the ferocious tiger.

The tiger started to snarl and pant and began to attack, running straight at her, when suddenly, almost upon her, she flung open her long black coat, revealing her beautiful young naked body.

John's eyes popped as the tiger stopped dead in its tracks, dropped to the floor like a cuddly Tigger toy, meekly crawled up to her and started licking her feet and ankles.

The tiger continued to lick and kiss her entire body for several minutes before resting its big ferocious head at her feet.

Bobby Roberts' jaw was on the floor having witnessed at first hand this reaction by one of his fiercest circus animals.

He turned to John and said, 'I've never seen anything like that in my entire circus life. How can you possibly top that?'

John replied, 'Easy peasy!

Just you get that tiger out of the way and I'll show you!'

Damn Lies

• • •

Two old codgers, Bill and Sid, would meet up in the park every day to feed the wild pigeons, watch the squirrels and discuss issues like global warming.

One day old Bill didn't show up. Sid didn't think much about it at the time, but figured maybe he had a cold or something.

However, after Bill hadn't appeared at the park for a week or so, Sid became worried.

The only time they'd ever got together was at the park, and Sid didn't know his friend's surname or where he lived, so he was unable to find out what had happened to him.

A month or so had passed, and Sid figured he had seen the last of old Bill, when out of the blue, one day Sid approached the park and lo and behold, there sitting on their park bench was Bill!

Sid was very excited and happy to see his friend, and he told him so.

'For goodness' sake, Bill, where in hell's name have you been?'

Bill replied, 'I've been in the Bar L.'

'Jail?' responded Sid. 'You've been in the jail? What in the world did you do, man?'

'Well,' Bill said. 'D'you know Sally, the cute little blonde waitress in the Asda coffee shop where I sometimes go?'

'Yeah,' replied Sid, 'I remember her. What about her?'

'Well, she filed rape charges against me, and at eighty-nine years old, I was just so proud that when I went into court for my trial, I pleaded guilty right away.'

'So you got locked up for rape?' asked Sid.

'Naw!' replied Bill, with more than a hint of disappointment in his voice.

'The bloody judge called me a liar and gave me thirty days for perjury.'

Naughty Neighbours

· · ·

During my twenty-nine-year police career I saw some disturbing and horrific sights, however they were nothing in comparison to what I was about to witness on several occasions in the one week.

I was working an early-shift week, having to rise with the alarm going off each morning at five o'clock.

After a quick shave, I got dressed and switched on the kettle for the obligatory early-morning 'wake me up' coffee, before making my way to the front door to collect the even earlier milk delivery on my doorstep.

By pure coincidence, for the umpteenth time that week, I opened my front door a split second before my neighbour, directly opposite, who once again appeared wearing a very low-cut, short see-through negligee, exposing dark, erect nipples and gold coloured high-heeled shoes.

Very fetching, I thought, and possibly a sexual turn-on for many people!

However, it was not for me. I felt I had to act responsibly so I put my police face and head on and called over,

'Here, George! One of these days you're going to get caught wearing your wife's clothes!'

Driving by Braille

...

One day I was out with my old mate Jimmy Clark, and we were driving along on our way to the Retired Police Officers' Association meeting.

We were both wearing our prescription spectacles.

As we drove along the road, chatting away, we approached a crossroad junction controlled by automatic traffic signals.

The traffic light was showing red, but Jimmy failed to comply with it and drove straight through.

I sat there in the passenger seat and thought to myself, 'I must be losing it here! I could have sworn he just drove through a red traffic light.'

After a few more minutes, we approached another crossroad junction where the traffic light was showing red, and just like the last one, Jimmy drove straight through it, failing to comply again.

This time, sitting in the passenger seat, I was almost certain that the traffic light had been red, but was also concerned that Jimmy might be seeing things.

I was becoming very anxious and nervy, so I decided to pay closer attention at the next junction. Sure enough, the light was definitely showing red and, without any attempt to slow down or stop, Jimmy drove right through it.

I couldn't ignore it any more, so I said, 'Jimmy! Did you know that you've failed to comply with three red lights in a row, each time driving straight through the junction? You could have killed the both of us!'

Jimmy turned to face me with a stunned expression on his face and said:

'Oh shit! I take it I'm driving then?'

The Moon Walk

· · ·

This is one of these wee stories you come across from time to time that is very interesting and allegedly true . . . Honest!

Apparently on July 20, 1969, when American astronaut Neil Armstrong, the commander of the Apollo 11 Lunar module, was about to make history by being the first person to set foot on the moon, his first words were immortalized as, 'That's one small step for a man, one giant leap for mankind.' These words were televised to Earth to be heard by millions all around the world.

However, just before he re-entered the module, he allegedly made the enigmatic remark, 'Good luck, Mr Gorsky.'

Many people at NASA naturally assumed it was a casual remark directed at some rival Soviet cosmonaut and so didn't pay too much attention to it at the time, but upon checking out the remark later, it appeared there was no Mr Gorsky in either the Russian or American space programmes.

Over the next few years, many people questioned Armstrong as to who the 'Good luck, Mr Gorsky' statement had been aimed at, but Armstrong remained tight-lipped, and would always smile, before declining to reply.

During another public appearance by Neil Armstrong on July 5, 1995, while being interviewed following a recent speech, a reporter made reference to the twenty-six-year-old question that Armstrong had never fully explained.

This time Armstrong finally responded.

The Mr Gorsky referred to in his remark had died, so he felt the question could now be addressed.

It appears that in 1938, when Armstrong was a young boy in a small Midwest town, he was outside in the back yard playing baseball with a friend, when the ball landed in his neighbour's yard, near to the bedroom window.

His neighbours at this time were Mr and Mrs Gorsky.

As Armstrong bent down to retrieve his ball, he heard Mrs Gorsky shouting at her husband.

'Sex! You want sex? You'll get sex when the kid next door walks on the moon!'

Dangerous Waters

· · ·

Normally, when you read a sign, or are told that 'these waters are dangerous', you automatically think: sharks! But not this time.

Apparently, fire authorities in California found a male corpse in a burned-out section of a forest while assessing the damage done by a forest fire.

The deceased male was dressed in a full wet suit, complete with scuba-diving tanks on his back, flippers, and face mask.

A post-mortem examination revealed that the man had died, not from burns, but from massive internal injuries.

Dental records provided the police with a positive identification. Police investigators then set about trying to determine how a fully clothed deep-sea diver had ended up in the middle of a forest fire.

It was revealed that on the day of the fire, the man went diving off the coast, some twenty miles away from the location of the forest.

The fire fighters, seeking to control the fire as quickly as possible, had called in a fleet of helicopters with very large dip buckets, so that the water could be collected from the ocean and emptied over the site of the forest fire.

You guessed it!

One minute our deep-sea diver was making out like Flipper in the Pacific, and the next he was doing the breast stroke in a fire dip bucket 300 feet up in the air.

Some days it just doesn't pay to get out of bed.

Donnie the Undertaker

· · ·

Big Donnie Henderson was on duty in his new career as assistant undertaker to a funeral director when a man who had just died was delivered to the mortuary by former colleagues John Davie and Leslie Rose.

The deceased was wearing an expensive, immaculately tailored black suit, when he suffered a fatal heart attack.

Donnie spoke with the deceased's wife and asked her how she would like the body to be dressed, pointing out that he looked very smart in the black suit that he was already wearing.

The widow, however, replied that she always felt her husband appeared at his best when dressed in blue, and it was therefore her preference for him to wear a blue suit.

She then presented Donnie with a blank cheque and said, 'I don't care how much it costs, but please have my husband dressed in a blue suit for the friends and family viewing.'

The woman returned the following day for the viewing and, to her amazement, she found her husband smartly dressed in a Ralph Slater blue suit with a subtle chalk stripe. It was a perfect fit.

She turned to Donnie with a tear in her eye and said, 'Whatever this cost, it was well worth it. I'm totally satisfied that you've done an excellent job and I'm very grateful to you. How much did you have to spend?'

To her complete and utter surprise, big Donnie replied, 'Nuthin'!' and returned her blank cheque. 'Not a penny, hen. There was absolutely no charge involved.'

'No really, you must allow me to compensate you for the cost of that exquisite blue suit!' she said.

'Honestly, hen,' Donnie said, 'it cost nuthin'. You see, after you left yesterday, another deceased gentleman, about your husband's size and build, was brought into the parlour and by sheer coincidence, he was wearing an attractive blue suit. So I asked his wife if she minded him going to his grave wearing a black suit instead of his blue one, and she replied it would make no difference to her, so long as he looked presentable.'

'So are you telling me you went to all the bother of stripping them both and changing over their suits?' she asked, impressed by the service provided.

'Don't be silly, hen,' responded Donnie. 'I just switched their heids roun'!'

Game On

...

Several of my police colleagues who lived and died for their Saturday morning round of golf were disappointed when one of the group was transferred to another division. It wasn't going to be the same without him.

A young policewoman was promoted into his position.

One morning during a coffee break, she heard the guys talking about their usual Saturday golf game and how they needed another player to make up the four, and said, 'I didn't tell you, but I used to play on my golf team at college and I was considered quite good. Would you mind if I replaced him and joined you for a game next week?'

The three cops looked at each other, none of them wanting to answer 'yes', but she had put them into am awkward position.

Finally, one of them agreed, but he pointed out that they started about 6.30a.m., thinking that the early tee-off time would discourage her.

The policewoman thought for a moment, before asking if she could be up to fifteen minutes late.

Her colleagues rolled their eyes, but reluctantly agreed to her request. 'Good!' she said. 'Then I'll be there at 6.30 or 6.45 at the latest.

The following Saturday, she showed up at 6.30 sharp and promptly beat all three of them with an impressive two-under-par round. She was very pleasant and good fun and the guys were suitably impressed.

Back at the clubhouse, they congratulated her and

invited her to play the following week. She smiled and replied, 'Okay. But as we agreed, I'll be there at 6.30 or 6.45.'

The next week she again showed up at 6.30 sharp. Only on this occasion, she brought her left-handed clubs to play.

Her police colleagues were speechless as she beat them with an even-par round, despite playing with her off-hand.

They were totally amazed, but suspected she was trying to make them look bad by beating them left-handed. They just couldn't figure her out, as she again was very pleasant and didn't seem to be deliberately trying to embarrass them.

Afterwards, they duly invited her back to play again, each of them desperate to beat her.

On the third week, the guys had their game faces on. However, this time, she was fifteen minutes late, which made them irritable.

This time she changed back to playing right-handed, and only just managed to beat them.

The guys discussed her late arrival and put it down to petty gamesmanship on her part. But she was so gracious and complimentary about how they each played that they couldn't hold a grudge.

Back at the clubhouse, all three guys were totally confused. This policewoman was a complete puzzle that none of them could work out. Finally, after a few beers, one of the cops asked her point blank:

'Tell me something. How do you decide if you're going to play right-handed or left-handed?'

The policewoman blushed, then grinned like a 'Cheshire cat'. 'That's easy,' she said. 'When my father taught me to play, I learned from an early age that I was ambidextrous. I liked to switch my game back and forth. Then, when I got married, I found out that my new husband likes to sleep in the nude. From that day, I developed a silly habit. Every morning, before I left the house for golf practice, I would pull the bed covers back and if his manhood was pointing to the right, I would golf right-handed, and if it was pointing to the left, I golfed left-handed.'

Her colleagues thought this explanation was hysterical.

Amazed at this bizarre information, one of the cops couldn't resist asking the obvious: 'But what if it's pointing straight up in the air?'

She looked straight into his eyes and said with a wicked grin on her face, 'Well, that's when I'm fifteen minutes late!'

True Crime

. . .

A male walked into an American fast-food diner where four police officers were eating and casually walked over to where they were seated.

He then produced a concealed firearm from under his coat and began firing it, killing all four officers, while they sat at their table. He then fled the crime scene.

One of the police officers was shot eight times, including once to the back of his head at close range. Another was shot a total of five times.

An immediate state-wide manhunt was begun for the murder suspect, who was at large, armed and dangerous.

The suspect was traced to a wooded area, where he immediately opened fire at the police. A team of highly trained firearm officers returned fire, hitting the suspect sixty-eight times.

The liberal-minded members of the media were outraged and asked the officer in charge, Sheriff Grady Judd, why they'd shot the suspect sixty-eight times.

Sheriff Judd replied forthrightly, with classic confidence,

'Cause that was all the ammunition we had with us!'

Did I Hear Right?

. . .

Wee Dougie, an unemployed Glesca punter, was nearing the end of another long, arduous day of sitting in his near-empty local pub in Govan, trying to pick a winner for the next televised horse race.

As he sat there alone, pondering over his choice and talking gibberish to himself, having swallowed a few Buckfast wines, as was the norm, the door opened and a short, fat, well-dressed gay man entered the hostelry, walked right up to the bar and sat down next to him.

Several drinks later, the gay man leaned over towards wee Dougie and whispered discreetly in his ear, 'Would you like a blowjob?'

Wee Dougie responded by jumping off his bar stool with rage in his eyes and promptly punching the gay man right off his stool, where he then proceeded to knock sixteen colours of shit out of him.

(That's nine more than a rainbow!)

He then grabbed him by the arse of his trousers and the neck of his jacket and frogmarched him out of the pub, leaving him battered and bruised in the street, before returning to his seat at the bar.

Not entirely amazed at what had just occurred, the barman quickly brought over another glass of Buckie to Dougie and said, 'Here, wee man, I've never seen you react as badly as that before. What in the hell did he say to you?'

Dougie thought for a moment, trying to recollect what he'd heard, before shaking his head and replying, 'Ah'm no' very sure, Tam, but it definitely sounded like he was trying to offer me a job!'

Mistaken ID

· · ·

All NHS hospital regulations require a wheelchair to be available for patients being discharged. However, while working as a student nurse, my sister Kim found an elderly gentleman already dressed and sitting on the bed with a suitcase at his feet.

As she approached him, he vehemently insisted that he didn't require her assistance to leave the hospital.

After making him aware that rules were rules, he reluctantly succumbed to her charm and let her push him in a wheelchair to the elevator.

On the way down she asked him if any of his family was meeting with him.

'I don't know,' he said.

'Well, what about your wife?' she asked.

The elderly gentleman looked at her with a puzzled expression on his face and said, 'My wife? She's still upstairs in the bathroom changing out of her hospital gown.'

Glesca Weans!

• • •

I was told this story by an ex-cop who is now a fully fledged pastor of a local church in the area where he worked as a police officer. Only a child from Glasgow could think of it.

He was testing the children in his local Sunday school class to see if they understood the concept of how to get to Heaven.

He asked them, 'If I was to sell my luxury house and my fancy sports car, had a big car boot sale, and gave all my money to the church, do you think that would get me into Heaven?'

'NO!' the children answered.

'Well, what if I cleaned the church every day, cut the grass, pruned the roses, and kept all the paths neat and tidy, do you think that would get me into Heaven?'

Again, their resounding answer was, 'NO!'

By now he was starting to feel extremely relaxed and good about his class. Smiling like a Cheshire cat in anticipation of the outcome, he continued.

'Well, then, if I was kind to animals and gave sweets to all the boys and girls present within the Sunday school today, and bought flowers for my lovely wife, would that get me into Heaven?'

Again, they all responded in unison with an emphatic, 'NO!'

He was just bursting with pride for them.

'Well,' he continued, 'then how will I get into Heaven?'

At that a six-year-old boy from the local housing scheme threw his hand up in the air.

'Tommy?' he said, keen to hear the answer.

Tommy shouted out with excitement in his young voice, 'Ye've got tae be deid first, ya bam!'

Harry's Classified Ads

· · ·

FREE YORKSHIRE TERRIER CALLED JOCK. Eight years old. Hateful little bastard. Bites everything and anything! Loves postmen, but generally will try to bite anyone.

Lost in Translation!

...

This was sent to me in a text. Very moving.

When you are sad . . . I will dry your tears.
When you are scared . . . I will comfort your fears.
When you are worried . . . I will give you hope.
When you are confused . . . I will help you cope.
And when you are lost and can't see the light . . . I shall be your beacon, shining ever so bright.
This is my oath, I pledge till the end.
Why, you may ask? . . . Because you're my friend.

A few days later, a police colleague sent me the Glesca version.

When ye are sad . . . I'll help ye get pished, then we'll get the bugger that upset ye.
When ye are blue . . . I will try to dislodge whatever it is that's choking ye, whether ye want me tae or not.
When ye are scared . . . I'll rip the pish right oot o' ye every chance ah get until ye're not.
When ye are worried . . . I'll tell ye how much worser it could be until ye stop moaning and start laughing.
When ye are sick . . . Stay the hell away fae me. Ah don't want tae catch it aff ye.
When ye fall . . . I'll laugh ma frigging heid aff, then help ye up.
This is my oath. I pledge it for a while. Why, ye might ask? . . . Because ye make me smile!

The Meaning of AH

· · ·

A traffic cop stopped a driver for failing to stop at a red light.

The driver, a real idiot, got out of his car and ran towards the police officer, demanding to know why he was being harassed by the 'Gestapo'.

The police officer informed him about the red light violation. The driver instantly went off on a tirade of abuse, questioning the marital status of the officer's parents, his sexual orientation, and so on, in rather explicit terms. This tirade went on for a few moments, as the officer calmly wrote out the ticket without saying anything.

When he was finished writing the ticket he added 'AH' in the lower-right corner of the narrative portion of the ticket. He then handed the ticket to the driver for his signature.

The driver signed the ticket and when presented with his copy, he pointed to the 'AH', demanding an explanation.

The police officer said, 'That's so when we go to court, I'll remember that you were an asshole!'

Three months later they were in court and the driver was about to lose his licence for having such a bad driving record, but had hired a top defence lawyer to represent him.

In the witness box, the officer testified to seeing the driver fail to comply with the red light.

Under cross-examination, the defence lawyer asked, 'Officer, is this the Fixed Penalty Notice that you issued to my client?'

The officer replied, 'Yes sir.'

The lawyer then asked, 'Is there any particular marking or notation on this ticket that you don't normally make?'

'Yes sir,' he replied. 'In the lower-right corner of the narrative section, I've added "AH" and underlined it.'

The lawyer then asked the officer to explain what 'AH' stood for.

'Aggressive and Hostile, sir,' he replied.

'Aggressive and Hostile?' repeated the lawyer.

'Yes sir,' responded the officer.

The lawyer paused for a moment, picked up the ticket for another look and said, 'Officer, are you sure it doesn't stand for Asshole?'

To which the officer replied with a wry smile. 'Well, sir, you would appear to know your client much better than I do!'

Sheep Shagging Mystery

• • •

Dougal was stationed for some time away in the outpost of Meldrum in Aberdeenshire. Being a section station, there were some times of day when only one polis was on duty.

One night when he was on duty alone, he received a call reporting that there was a man crawling down Main Street.

Sure enough, when he went to investigate, there was one of the locals, Willie MacKay, pissed out of his mind, crawling along the roadside totally oblivious to the rest of the world.

Dougal got him into the car and carted him off to the jail 'for his own safety', as per the Aberdeen Instruction Manual.

However, the ruling stated that you NEVER put a drunk into a cell alone before removing the old army style blanket that was supplied for creature comfort.

Unfortunately, while placing wee Willie into the cell, the phone rang again, with the caller reporting an incident at a local colliery.

Dougal locked him up and hurried away to attend the latest incident, forgetting to remove the blanket, or take the time to note his particulars in the custody book.

As a result, having dealt with the other incident, Dougal completely forgot about wee Willie and drove home to have his break, before returning to the station, where he was met by the station sergeant looking for an update on what was happening in the metropolis.

It was only then that Dougal remembered wee Willie was still in the station cell.

When he went to get him out, Willie had all the hairs from the army blanket sticking to his three days' beard growth.

'Whit am ah in here for?' he asked.

At which point Dougal asked him if he had been drinking in one of the local pubs that bordered a farmer's field.

'Aye! Ah wiz,' Willie replied. 'Whit's that goat tae dae wi' it?'

At that Dougal proceeded to tell him that he had been apprehended for sheep shagging and went on to show him the wool, (from the blanket) sticking to his beard and charged him accordingly.

He went on to advise Willie that he should contact the local doctor, who Dougal was friendly with, to make him aware of what was going on, should Willie require to attend the surgery.

Willie was later released and nothing more was heard of the experience till one of Dougal's colleagues went to serve the copy complaint on Willie for his appearance at court.

The serving officer carried this out as per the police instruction manual, unaware of Willie having been locked up.

Wee Willie's wife then asked the officer what Willie had been charged with on the big night, so he read the summary to her, informing her that Willie had been drunk and incapable.

'Thank gidness for that!' she replied. 'That's a big weight aff ma mind, 'cause he's been pestering the life oot o' me wantin' tae go an' see the doacter because he wis caught sheep worrying.'

On hearing her remark, the officer repeated the charge of drunk and incapable as listed in the copy complaint, pointing out that there was no mention of the sheep worrying.

However, Willie's wife had to have the last word and she replied, 'Ye ken this, polis. In ma ain heart ah kent it wid be fine that ma Willie hudnae been oot worryin' sheep, cause ah ken for sure he didnae huv his false teeth in that nicht!'

It must be an Aberdonian custom, or maybe just a loophole for the defence to argue that one must have false teeth in, in order to commit the crime of worrying sheep!

Don't ask – I've absolutely no idea why his teeth would make a difference . . .

Unless he gave the sheep a love bite first!

The Honeymoon
. . .

I really enjoyed this when it was sent to me by a colleague and had to include it for a laugh!

Gavin Hill, a retired police officer, and his wife Mary were on a second honeymoon, near Transylvania, Romania, driving along a rather deserted country road late at night, when it started raining very heavily.

Gavin could barely see the road in front of him, when suddenly the car skidded out of control. Gavin used all his police driving skills as he attempted to steer the car, but to no avail. As a result the car swerved and collided with a tree.

Moments later, having struck the windscreen, Gavin shook his head to clear his sight. Dazed and concussed, he looked over at the passenger seat and saw Mary lying there unconscious, with her head bleeding profusely from her injuries.

Despite the heavy rainfall and unfamiliar landscape, Gavin's natural instincts were to get Mary some urgent medical assistance.

He carefully picked her up and began to trudge along the road. After a short while, he noticed a light in the distance coming from a large house. He approached the door and knocked on it.

The door was opened by a small, hunched man. Gavin immediately blurted out, 'Help me, please, my name is Gavin Hill, and this is my wife, Mary. We've been involved in a road accident, and my wife has been seriously injured. Can I please use your telephone to call an ambulance?'

'I'm sorry,' replied the hunchback, 'we don't have a

telephone, but my master is a doctor, maybe he can assist you!' At that he opened the door wider. 'Come in and I will inform him of your presence!'

A few moments later an older man walked into the room where Gavin and Mary were waiting and after introducing himself he said, 'I'm afraid my butler Igor may have misled you. I am not a medical doctor, I am a scientist. However, I do have some basic medical training, so I will see what I can do for you.'

At that he turned to Igor and instructed him to bring them down to his laboratory.'

Igor picked up Mary and carried her downstairs, closely followed by Gavin.

Igor gently placed Mary on the table in the lab, at which point Gavin collapsed from sheer exhaustion, coupled with his own injuries, so Igor picked him up and placed him on an adjoining table next to Mary.

After a brief examination, Igor's master appeared worried. 'Things are very serious, Igor. We must prepare a blood transfusion immediately.'

Igor and his master worked feverishly to administer emergency transfusions, but to no avail. Gavin and Mary Hill died on the operating tables.

The Hills' deaths upset Igor's master greatly.

Exhausted from his efforts to save them, he climbed the stairs to his oval conservatory, and his grand piano. For it is there that he always found solace.

He sat down on his stool, cracked his fingers and began to play the most stirring, haunting of tunes. The melody found every room of the house.

Meanwhile, Igor was still in the lab cleaning up when his eyes caught a sudden movement, and noticed the fingers on Mary's hand twitching, keeping time with the haunting piano music. Stunned by this, he watched as Gavin's arm began to rise up, and wave, as if conducting every musical note! He was then further amazed as Mary and Gavin both sat up straight on the tables!

Unable to contain himself, Igor dashed up the stairs to the conservatory, burst in the door and shouted, 'Master, Master! The Hills are alive with the sound of music!'

(I am soooooo, soooooo sorry. But you really should've seen that coming!)

Family Reunion

. . .

A wee Glesca punter called up his son in London, the day before Christmas Eve, and announced, 'I hate to ruin your day, son, but I thought it was only right to tell you that after nearly fifty years of marital bliss, your mother and I are getting divorced.

'What? Dad, what are you talking about?' the son asked.

'It's simple, son, we can't stand the sight of each other any longer,' the father said. 'We're sick to the back teeth with each other and I'm fed up living a lie, so you can call your sister in Corby and tell her.'

Shocked by this news, the son called his sister, who exploded over the phone. 'Like hell they're getting divorced!' she bawled. 'You just leave this to me!'

She quickly got on the phone to Glasgow and screamed at her father, 'You are NOT getting divorced. So don't you dare do a single thing until I get there. I'm coming up to Glasgow along with Jack, and we'll both be there tomorrow. Until then, just wait for us and don't do anything silly. Do you hear what I'm saying, Dad?'

'I hear you, hen!' he replied.

At that, she hung up the phone.

The Glesca punter replaced his phone, turned to his wife and said, 'That's it arranged, hen! They're both travelling up for Christmas, and they're paying for it themselves for a change!'

Wife Tells All!

• • •

While engaged in motorway patrol duty, I pulled over a speeding car onto the hard shoulder.

I approached the car and said to the driver, 'I've just clocked you driving at ninety miles per hour.'

The driver replied, 'I'm very sorry, Officer, but it's a new car and I'm using the cruise control. I'm positive I set it at sixty. Maybe your radar equipment needs to be checked!'

At that, his wife in the passenger seat said, 'Now, now, darling, don't be silly, you know fine well that this new car doesn't have cruise control.'

On hearing this, I wrote out the speed ticket and handed it to the driver, who looked over at his wife and said, 'For once, when I'm talking, can you please keep your big mouth shut?'

The wife smiled demurely and said, 'You should just be thankful that your radar detector went off when it did, or you would be getting charged for driving even faster.'

That said, I wrote out a second ticket for him having an illegal radar detector fitted to the car.

As I handed it over, the driver glowered at his wife and said through clenched teeth, 'Dammit, woman, can you not keep your big trap shut?'

Just then, I realised he wasn't wearing his safety belt and said, 'I've just noticed that you're not wearing a seat belt either, sir. That's another automatic fixed penalty fine.'

The driver then said, 'Well, Officer, I did have it on, but took it off when you pulled me over so that I could get my driving licence out of my back pocket!'

The wife piped up, 'Now, now, dear, you know fine well you didn't have your seat belt on. In fact, if truth be known, you never wear your seat belt when you're driving!'

This prompted me to consider issuing another penalty ticket, when the driver turned to his wife and growled, 'Why don't you just keep your mouth shut, you interfering old cow?' I looked over at the woman passenger and asked, 'Does he always talk to you like this, hen?'

To which she replied, 'Not normally, Officer. Only when he's drank too much whisky.'

Reg McKay Tribute

• • •

The last time I had lunch with my friend and fellow author Reg McKay in the Rogano, Exchange Place, we were having a laugh and I said, 'I picked up your latest book the other day – couldn't put it down.'

Before I could deliver the punchline, he reacted first. 'Don't tell me they're still putting superglue on the book covers!'

Not only one of Scotland's great crime writers, he was also a very quick witted and funny guy.

However, my favourite story about Reg McKay was nothing to do with his best-selling crime books, but an impromptu comment that came from Reg himself and was related to me by his good friend Tony Higgins during the funeral service.

Apparently while walking around Barshaw Park in Paisley together, Reg announced, in between cigarettes, that since the news about his terminal illness had been made public, he had been inundated with numerous offers from publishers for any forthcoming books he was writing.

'D'you know, Tony,' he'd said, 'I've had that many offers in the past few weeks, I wish tae fuck I had announced I was dying two years ago!'

That was the measure of the man, that he could see humour in his own tragic circumstances and make light of it.

RIP Reg McKay.

The Origin of Names

· · ·

I suppose it was a celebrity thing a while back, but the HOW and the WHY only came to light recently, when one of them broke the silence and decided to explain the reasoning behind it.

The Beckhams started the trend when they named their first-born child Brooklyn, stating it was the place where he was conceived. If that is true, thank goodness they didn't decide on a dirty weekend in Peckham!

This was followed up with wee brother Cruz. I think they were aboard the Love Boat cruise ship when they came up with that one! And by the way, this was BTC . . . Before Tom Cruise!

A dangerous precedent to start, I think. Just ask Broom Cupboard Becker! (Boris's love child) and Daylight Robbery (that's a joke, his real name was Bank!), Ronald Biggs' nephew.

We also have the video exhibitionist Paris Hilton, possibly conceived in the Hilton Paris (just a rough guess); Chelsea Clinton (old Bill gets about) and Mercedes Ruehl (whose father was an FBI agent who lived out of his car, allegedly).

Here's a thought – what about Madonna's daughter Lourdes? How did that one come about? I'm not even going to go there.

Others have included River Phoenix (a water baby, no doubt), Minnie Driver (father's name Lawrie perhaps?), Blanket Jackson (I think that was just a big cover-up, Michael!) and just to show he wasn't the only Jackson who was a few sandwiches short of a picnic, his brother Jermaine named his wean Jermajesty. Nutty or what?

Then there's Rumer Willis (no truth in that one then?) and Noel Gallagher (conceived at Christmas! I think if they'd named him Santa, it would have helped his career big time!)

You need to ask yourself, 'Where did this lot come from?' They must have been high on drugs. I mean, Whoopi Goldberg, Fifi Trixibelle Geldof, Zowie Bowie and big Tam the Bam (a popular choice of name for a Glesca punter from Govan).

The more I look into this, the worse it gets. Step forward the classic Moon Unit and his sister Diva Thin Muffin, the offspring of Frank Zappa! Frank? What the hell were you taking when you named these two wee souls? Yer heid must have been puggled!

I wonder if Diva Muffin is any relation to Dunkin Donuts?

And we have to mention Bono and the Edge from U2. They both assumed these weird stage names, but why lumber their kids with Memphis Eve and Blue Angel respectively?

Sounds like a right heavy cocktail hour if you ask me.

Personally, I'd blame burst condoms. No, that's not another name, it's a product that failed their amorous fathers at a very specific time.

Actor Forest Whitaker came up with the name Ocean for his son. This was apparently a spontaneous outburst when he was present at his wife's side, at the exact moment her waters broke. Splassshhhh!

No sooner are you getting used to this lot, when along comes the Naked Chef himself, Jamie Oliver and his offspring, Poppy, Daisy, followed by the latest addition, Blossom Petal. All blooming girls, pardon the pun, and all conceived in a big flower bed, no doubt.

What next? Pansy, Peat and the unplanned Dandy Lion! You don't need a nursery for this lot. You need a garden centre!

Come to think of it, maybe they were all conceived on a visit to B & Q! Pure 'pukka', Jamie boy!

Maybe the Native American had a big influence over how they went about picking names.

Apparently, they decided to name their children according to the first thing they saw immediately after the baby was born.

I mean to say, they had some right belters as well. Crazy Horse, Full Moon, White Cloud and the triplets, Running Water, Running Bear and Big Brown Bear. If there had been quads, they might have named the fourth one Running Away From Big Brown Bear!

And there are also the sisters, or squaws, born into the tribe, like Blue Moon, Bright Sky and the ones they don't talk about: Pissing With Rain, Passing Wind, and Dog Poo!

I reckon that even old Desmond Tutu came from a long line of ballet dancers! What do you think?

The Celts are not averse to doing something similar. I was over in Ireland recently and was introduced to Pat McGroin (a physiotherapist), Phil McAvity (went on to sell wall insulation), and Finbarrack O'Bamma. Oh, and not forgetting those well-known Irish barbers, Tom O'Hawk and Kurt M'hair!

Gone are the traditional hand-me-down family names like Thomas, Archibald, William, Robert, Isobel, Elizabeth and Josephine, which we all took great delight in shortening to Tam, Archie, Willie, Rab, Bel, Liz and Josie.

Even my own mother-in-law was christened Annie, but throughout her entire childhood and adult life, her parents, close relatives and friends called her May.

Why not just name her May to start with, like when you filled out her birth certificate? Mind you, bearing this in mind, everyone would probably have called her Annie!

And now, we have this ridiculous trend of 'crackpot' names escalating, where every single parent in a Glesca housing scheme has decided to follow suit.

'Let's no' name her jist yet, doll, finish aff yer glass o' voddie and we'll smoke anither spliff first. Clear oor minds! Then we'll pick a right trendy, gallus name she'll be proud of.'

Only the other day I heard a young mother call out to her little girl, loud and clear, 'Princess Govan of the Cross McGinty! You get yer arse o'er here pronto, or else!'

Or else what? You'll hit her with a right stupid name?

Personally, I'm looking out for Blyth Wood (the prostitute's favourite), Garth Amlock (from the housing schemes), Fergus Lee-Park (an Asian immigrant born in Paisley), Chic Currie (a popular Glesca/Asian name), and Ford Van-Transit (his mammy gave birth to him on her way back from Amsterdam).

I suppose if we think about it, it could've started with the first test-tube babies!

Anybody know a Pyrex Bowles? Or a Tippi Tupperware?

What about the artificial insemination twins, Sperm and Donna?

The Scottish Siamese twins, Oor Wullie and Oor Boaby.

As for me and all your fancy names, I still prefer the old favourite Glesca term of endearment when drunk, wi' a doner kebab in one's hand: 'Ur ye awright there, my wee China?'

And Finally

· · ·

Having suffered from depression for several months after an unfortunate accident, whereby a man had to have his arm amputated from above his elbow, he decided he'd had enough of being unable to hug his wife, tie his shoe laces, use a knife and fork at the same time, and so on. He felt his life was over.

The following day, he made his way up to the Erskine Bridge and climbed over the barrier.

As he stood on the edge, preparing to throw himself off, his attention was drawn to a man with no arms, skipping along the road towards him.

He watched in disbelief as the armless man got closer, apparently laughing ecstatically to himself and dancing some kind of jig!

It made him think about how ungrateful he was to be feeling sorry for himself. Here was a man with no arms at all! At least he still had the use of one arm.

This appeared like a message to him that hit home to his conscience, prompting him to humbly ask, 'You have no arms, so how come you appear to be extremely happy, laughing hysterically to yourself, while dancing a jig?'

To which the man with no arms loudly replied: 'ITCHY ARSE!'

Harry Says, 'Share With Me!'

...

Former Police Officer Harry Morris and now the author of the popular 'Harry the Polis' series of books is planning to publish book number nine in the series of funny short polis stories.

Harry the Polis: Glesca Polis at Their Best

He would like to extend an invitation to all serving and retired polis, along with all F.S.O. staff, to contribute a story to future publications and allow the popular series to continue.

Stories must be of a humorous nature and can even be a short scenario of an incident that you would like the author to expand upon. (All characters' names will be changed.)

We are all very much aware of the seriousness and important side of the job when serving the public. That's why the humour we enjoyed in our everyday police duties was a very important feature of our work.

So why not share it with your colleagues and the public by giving everyone a laugh, as opposed to reading about the horrific day-to-day crimes that are reported daily in the press and forced upon us in the news. Everybody likes a right good laugh.

Just send either stories, poems, anecdotes, jokes or tales to:
harry@harrythepolis.com
Website: www.harrythepolis.com

The author will be sure to credit you with your submission. However, if you wish to remain anonymous, this will also be respected by the author. The main objective is not to make fun of the police, but to write about the humour we all enjoyed.

So why not start writing and let me hear from you. We all have a funny story we've been involved in, so why not share it?

Every attempt is made to identify the author of any material submitted and used.

NEXT PUBLICATION IN THE SERIES: VOLUME 9

GLESCA POLIS AT THEIR BEST!

Thank You

...

Here's hoping you enjoyed perusing through another book of short stories in the latest 'Harry the Polis' series of light-hearted fun and laughter. As always, I have thoroughly enjoyed writing, editing and compiling these stories over the past years.

To all my friends and former colleagues, past, present and dead, coupled with those who are young, not so young, and who will sign on for a career as a future police officer, I would offer you my invaluable experience and advice.

At all times, try and use common sense when dealing with a particular incident and don't ever be afraid to show your compassion – and most of all, use your discretion. It's you who decides whether a warning will suffice in certain incidents.

Lastly, and most importantly, if you can't take a joke and laugh at yourself, then you should leave that particular job to others . . . especially me and my many readers, of course!

Acknowledgements

* * *

Harry Morris would like to extend his sincere appreciation to Peter Conoboy, Alec Craig, Ian Taylor, Tom Palmer, Robert Bell, John Baird and all those uniformed senior officers who just wish to remain anonymous (in case it affects their future promotion prospects). Your contributions were appreciated, so I hope I did them justice.

A special thank you to everyone at Black & White Publishing, without whose help and support I would have been committed long ago

Contact Details

• • •

www.harrythepolis.com

harry@harrythepolis.com

Harry Morris, aka 'Harry the Polis', all-round good guy, is available for Stand-Up Humour, Storytelling, Babysitting, Guest Speaking, Airport Runs, and Script / Sketch Writing.

All enquiries to info@harrythepolis.com

Harry Morris is a member of the Society of Authors, a member of Equity and is also registered with the Scottish Book Trust for Live Literature Events and workshops.